PUSHING THE LIMITS

Pushing the Limits

disabled
dykes
produce
culture

edited by Shelley Tremain

CANADIAN CATALOGUING IN PUBLICATION DATA

Main entry under title:
Pushing the limits
ISBN 0-88961-218-8
1. Lesbians' writings, Canadian (English) .* 2. Lesbians' writings, American.
3. Canadian literature (English) — 20th century.* 4. American literature — 20th
century. 5. Lesbianism — Literary collections. 6. Handicapped — Literary
collections. 7. Art, Canadian. 8. Art, American. 9. Art Modern — 20th Century
— Canada. 10. Art, Modern — 20th century — United States. 11. Lesbianism
in art. 12. Handicapped in art. I Tremain, Shelley.

PS8235.L47P87 1996   C810.8'0353   C95-932805-X
PR9194.5.L47P87 1996

Cover art: "Congress of Vienna, 1880" (charcoal, graphite, and beeswax on
paper, 50" w x 41.5" h) by Julia Patterson
Cover design: Sandra Haar
Editor: Jacquie Buncel
Copy editor: Lynda Nancoo
Author photograph: Moe Laverty

Printed and bound Canada.
1 2 3 4 5   2000 1999 1998 1997 1996

Dedicated to the memory of

Kathleen Martindale

(April 4, 1947 — February 17, 1995)

Contents

Acknowledgements

Over the course of the four years during which I have worked on this anthology, many women have encouraged and supported me. I welcome the opportunity to publicly thank some of them here.

First, I would like to express my deep gratitude to Ann Decter and Martha Ayim, the managing editors at Women's Press with whom I worked closely. If I had been without recourse to Ann's practical wisdom, I would not have persevered with this project, nor would I have known when the time had come to let go of it. I am especially grateful to Martha for the way in which she directed the final stages of the book's production. She did so diligently, enthusiastically, and with the earnest that is characteristic of her.

I am indebted to Jacquie Buncel who edited many of the pieces in this collection. The anthology has benefitted from Jacquie's appreciation for the nuances of language, and I have benefitted from the advice and support which she generously gave me.

I want to thank Heather Guylar for the very effective way in which she has formatted, and laid out, the writing and the artwork that are included here.

My thanks to Lynda Nancoo who copy-edited the manuscript, and did so with great care.

Thanks to my dear friend Julia Patterson who produced the brilliant piece of artwork which appears on the front cover of the book. The evocative way in which Julia confronts oralist culture testifies to the cultural struggles of Hard-of-Hearing, oral Deaf, and Deaf, dykes.

Sandra Haar designed a striking cover on which to present Julia's piece. I wish to thank Sandra for that contribution to this project, as well as for her continued support of disabled dyke cultural work.

I greatly appreciate the ways in which Melody Burton, Kathleen Martindale's partner, and Debra Shogan, one of Kathleen's close friends, assisted me with the editorial work that was done on Kathleen's manuscript.

< 13 >

I want to send out thanks to all of the women — disabled and non-disabled, lesbian, two-spirited, transgendered, bi, and straight alike — who circulated various calls for submissions, posted them, read them on Toronto's CKLN 88.1 FM community radio station, or who otherwise birthed this anthology, especially: Jodi at *HIKANÉ*, Julia Patterson, Shahnaz Stri, Joanne Patterson, the editors of *DYKES, DISABILITY, AND STUFF*, Sherree Clark, Jane Field, Anita Block, Two Feathers, Judy Koch, Deborah Barretto, Jo Ann Chew, the staff at the Women's Bookstop in Hamilton, Fran Odette, and Barb Taylor.

Finally, I would like to honour all of the disabled dykes who responded to calls for submissions to this anthology. Despite the fact that few of them knew me, each one entrusted me with part of her life, entrusted me with it on the tacit understanding that I would do my utmost to safeguard its integrity. I sincerely hope that I have lived up to the expectations of every one of them.

Shelley Tremain
May 1996

< 14 >

We're Here. We're Disabled and Queer. Get Used to It.
Shelley Tremain

**"You look like a dyke, honey,
but you don't look disabled."**

When I told a gay male acquaintance of mine that this
anthology would soon be published, that is what he said to
me. Although he seemed to think that he had complimented
me, I certainly did not think he had done so. Now, I was
not at all surprised that he had made that sort of remark to
me. Since few persons recognize, and actually understand,
the ways in which I am routinely disabled, usually when I
come out as a disabled person to one who is non-disabled,
she or he either does not take me seriously, and thinks that
I have made a bad joke, or assumes that I seek some kind
of affirmation, reassures me that she or he would not have
suspected that I am disabled if I had not said so, and then
tells me that I "look normal." But, remarks like these are
reprehensible regardless of whether I am, or I am not,
accustomed to them. In order for one to make such a remark,
she or he must already hold discriminatory beliefs about, for
example, who counts as a disabled person, what disabled
persons look like, what kinds of lives we lead, and how we
wish to identify. In fact, the remark that my acquaintance
made to me crystallizes how a certain ableist notion which
pervades mainstream culture is recast, and reproduced within
lesbian, gay, and queer cultural contexts.

Amongst anti-ableist writers and activists, there is a con-
sensus that non-disabled persons generally regard disabled
persons as asexual beings. Although this falsehood degrades
all disabled persons, it has especially humiliating effects upon
disabled dykes. The reason it does so is this: if one assumes
that disabled persons are asexual, then one cannot conceive
the *existence* of disabled dykes. That is to say, if disabled

< 15 >

persons are regarded as asexual beings, and if dyke identities are *sexual* identities, then disabled dyke identities are a conceptual impossibility (do not exist). Apparently, the category of "disabled person," and the category of "dyke," are mutually exclusive ones: one is either a(n) (asexual) disabled person, or one is a (sexual) dyke. One might, of course, be neither a disabled person, nor a dyke; but one cannot, it seems, be both a disabled person *and* a dyke. Non-disabled dykes conceptually annihilate disabled dykes when they conceive of themselves as sexualized dykes and *de*-sexualize disabled dykes in order to subsume us in the always already desexualized, and racialized, category of "disabled women." When the straight (white) disabled women's movement obscures disabled dyke identities, and circulates that name ("disabled women") in order to appear as an unified movement, it too cancels our existence. Indeed, when, and if, straight disabled women refuse to acknowledge the specificity of disabled dyke identities, they actually *promote* the disableist lie that disabled persons are asexual beings and, hence, they unintentionally negate their own hetero-sexuality too.

I contend that the notion according to which disabled dykes do not exist currently *conditions* the ways in which dykes are represented in every sphere of lesbian cultural production, and in fact circumscribes what constitutes those cultures. Needless to say, the work of disabled dyke writers, artists, and photographers is not included in (non-disabled) lesbian anthologies, histories, or exhibitions. Moreover, the visual (for example, filmic, video, photographic) representations of lesbians which non-disabled dykes produce rarely, if ever, depict disabled dykes, our bodies, or our sexual practices; non-disabled lesbian literature does not include characters who are disabled dykes; nor do lesbian and feminist theories grapple with the ways in which ableism and disableism compound the effects of the lesbophobia, racism, anti-Semitism, classism, ageism, and sexism which disabled dykes variously face. Indeed, although so-called "cutting-edge" lesbian and feminist theorists recognize, and

< 16 >

interrogate, the ways in which complicated networks of social power constitute the categories of sex, gender, race, and sexuality, they uncritically accept the notions of "ability" and "disability" as prediscursive, ahistorical, and objective ones. Suffice it to say that inasmuch as feminist and queer theorists neglect to problematise the ways in which relations of power *naturalize* conceptions of ability and disability, ableism and disableism have already structured their work.

Certainly ableism structures lesbian, gay, and queer politics beyond the academy, where non-disabled dyke, fag, and queer activists do not organize against it. In fact, most non-disabled queers seem wholly uninterested in the struggles in which disabled dykes must engage in order to access allegedly "public" transit, or to find affordable, accessible housing, to obtain dyke-positive personal assistance and attendant services, or to resist the institutionalized power of non-disabled persons who attempt to incarcerate (that is, segregate) them in so-called "long-term care" facilities. From the perspective of most non-disabled queer activists, it seems, these struggles are not truly "political" ones, nor are they properly "queer" ones. Not surprisingly, due to the fact that the vast majority of non-disabled queers could not seem to care less about the living conditions of their disabled sisters, many disabled dykes feel forced to remain closeted, or to go back into the closet in order to safeguard their access to service-providers, as well as to ensure that members of disabled communities will be their political allies if, and when, they need advocacy, or support.

When non-disabled dyke theorists and activists represent disabled dykes at all, they do so in ways that demean some of the very dykes whom they exclude in the first place. Although non-disabled dyke cultural workers do not produce materials in formats which are accessible to blind dykes, and dykes who have low vision, nor organize events which are accessible to Deaf, and Hard-of-Hearing dykes, they repeatedly invoke, and malign, these disabled dykes in order to empower themselves. To put it bluntly, some of the most frequently used, and widely understood, linguistic practices

< 17 >

of dyke cultures (if not progressive movements, in general) are implicitly ableist, and disableist, ones.

Take, for instance, the ways in which the terms 'visible' and 'invisible' are currently used as metaphors in dyke, and queer, cultures. Within lesbian, gay, and queer cultures, to say that one is "visible" (that is, *seen*), is to imply that one is accounted for, recognized, acknowledged, and has community, as well as personal, pride; meanwhile, to say that one is "invisible" (that is, *not seen*), is to imply that one is not accounted for, not recognized/misrecognized, not acknowledged/ignored, and often also to imply that one is ashamed, embarrassed, self-loathing, in denial. Notice how these metaphors privilege *seeing* as that activity which enables one to produce the most reliable knowledge, where if one can *see* a given thing, then one can know the thing as it *really* is. In other words, one who can *see*, can produce knowledge; in contrast, one who *cannot see*, cannot produce knowledge. My argument is that insofar as these metaphors privilege sight in this way, and connote in the ways in which they do (that is, associate *seeing* with knowing, and *not seeing* with not knowing), they impact upon the self-esteem of blind dykes and dykes with low vision, in particular, and contribute to the social marginalization of blind persons, in general.

The metaphors of "voice" and "silence" (currently fashionable virtually *everywhere* in lesbian, feminist, and queer cultures) are also ones which demoralize disabled persons.[1] These metaphors are the historical legacies of oralist cultures, where one who *speaks* (or, "has a voice") is characterized as self-determining, liberated, and whole; meanwhile, one who does *not speak* (that is, "is silent," or "silenced") is represented as subjugated, captive, incomplete. As Julia Patterson's piece on the cover of *Pushing the Limits* evocatively suggests, these metaphors not only degrade Deaf and Hard-of-Hearing dykes, as well as other dykes whose language is not a spoken one, they also reinforce, and perpetuate, the ways in which Deaf culture is relegated to voice culture. In "Survival, Silence and the Obvious Remains," Frances Yip Hoi demonstrates a more politically astute way in which dykes, queers, and

< 18 >

feminists, could employ the metaphor of "silence." Drawing upon Foucauldian analyses into the disciplinary function of the confessional, Yip Hoi uses the term 'silence' in order to connote a form of *resistance* against discourses of disclosure, discourses in which the activity of *speaking*, an activity that is claimed to enable self-understanding, to liberate, and to "heal," actually functions in the service of particular forms of power that control socially subordinated women (especially disabled dykes, First Nations' women, Black women, women of colour, poor women, and disabled straight women). I want to suggest that if hearing dykes, queers, and feminists, were to reinscribe the metaphor of "silence" in the way in which Yip Hoi does here, then they would not only begin to redress harms that they have inflicted upon the Deaf community, but could also develop fresh, new ways in which to resist forms of social power that pathologize theexperiences of many women in order to therapize them.

Despite the fact that many non-disabled persons trivialize the disputes surrounding ableist language, and dismiss them as mere forays into "political correctness,"[2] those of us who do anti-ableist work believe that these debates are subversive ones. Historically, disabled persons have been variously marked as subhuman, evil, cursed, brave, and pitiful. Although every one of these age-old stereotypes persists in the present in one form or another there are also new ways in which disabled persons are categorized and stigmatized. Over the last centuries, that is, disabled persons living in industrialized countries have been forced to identify with an ever-increasing array of medical and administrative classifications, ones which dehumanize them (even though they do not seem as if they do so), and which serve the economic and socio-political interests of non-disabled persons. The latest innovations of this seemingly innocuous form of power are terms such as 'physically challenged,' 'mentally challenged,' 'developmentally delayed,' and 'differently-abled,' the latter of which is the term that the supposedly accountable organizers of the Michigan Womyn's Music Festival have popularized, and which many non-disabled dykes have

< 19 >

uncritically embraced as one that disabled persons themselves have coined. For the record, then, I should point out
that insofar as this term positions so-called "able-bodied"
persons as the norm from which "differently-abled" persons
differ, it is an especially condescending, and pejorative
euphemism, one with which disabled persons repeatedly,
and consistently, refuse to identify. As a matter of fact, none
of the more than 50 disabled dykes from whom I received
over 150 submissions for this anthology referred to herself in
that way, nor even mentioned that term.

Nevertheless, I have had many experiences with non-disabled lovers, allies, and friends (not to mention, doctors,
physiotherapists, and social workers) which have demon-
strated to me that far too often non-disabled persons claim
to know what is in the best interests of disabled persons
better than do disabled persons themselves. So, I am certain
that there are many non-disabled dykes who would doubt
what I have just written, would argue that the term 'differently-abled' is a "positive" one, and, furthermore, would
question why the term 'disabled' is used in the title of this
book.[3] If you are a non-disabled dyke, and you fit this
description, I suggest that you consider whether you would
wish to be categorized a "differently-sexual" woman; indeed,
consider how you would feel if you were categorized to as
a "differently-sexed" person.

Within the terms of the anti-ableist discourse which I
endorse, the word 'disabled' does not imply that one is
"defective," "helpless," "child-like," "useless," or any other
epithet which has been directed at disabled persons in order
to justify the fact that we are disenfranchised. To the contrary,
when anti-ableist activists employ the term 'disabled' in the
way in which I am here,[4] we do so in order to indicate that
a given person is socially marginalized, and disempowered,
in relation to hegemonic societal norms about (for example)
what persons should look like, how they should behave, how
they should go from one place to another, and how they
should communicate. In other words, when anti-ableist activists use the term 'non-disabled' in the way in which I am

< 20 >

here, we do so in order to refer to persons who are privileged vis-à-vis this systemic form of power, as well as to situate ourselves at the centre of discourse, that is, to position ourselves as the norm.

Each of the contributors to this anthology demands to be acknowledged as a dyke, and as a disabled one. Insofar as these writers, visual artists, and musicians refuse to remain ignored, they *push the limits* of who counts as a dyke, what constitutes "lesbian experience," who engages in female same-sex erotic activity, and how. Their efforts to expand an ableist category (namely, dyke) ought to be conceived as conceptually, and practically, continuous with the political and cultural movement that dykes of colour, working-class dykes, butch dykes, femmes, as well as two-spirited and transgendered women, have already initiated in order to counter the authoritative racist and classist ways in which dykes are represented. Needless to say, the work of these disabled dykes also implicitly challenges the white heterosexualism that dominates the disability rights movement, a movement which seldom aligns itself with queer struggles for justice in the institutional, symbolic-discursive, and social realms.

Let me make a few remarks about the way in which I have arranged the transgressive work which comprises this anthology. I have divided the anthology into nine sections, where each section is thematised around a word, or phrase, that signifies a way in which disabled dykes push the limits of the category of "dyke." Not coincidentally, I have arranged the sections in an order which suggests passage to consciousness — *political* consciousness — of oneself as a disabled dyke. Hence, the first section, "Searching," includes work which evokes struggles to embody an identity, struggles which arise, in part, due to the fact none of the identities which has so far been articulated seems to be an adequate one. "Becoming," the second section of the book, includes work which suggests movement from our past and present identities to future ones. Entitled "Loving," the writing in the third section confirms the knowledge that we have of ourselves

< 21 >

as sensuous, sexual, and sexy dykes. "Positioning" names the process of negotiation with non-disabled lovers, personal assistants, and so on, in which many of us must engage in order to secure our autonomy, dignity, and privacy. The title of the fifth section, "Enduring," signifies the fact that, as disabled dykes, we fight to live through the ways in which the medical establishment assaults our bodies, and our spirits. "Not Surrendering" includes work which articulates the idiosyncratic character of the homophobia, ableism, racism, oralism, and classism, that disabled dykes variously confront. The work included in "Testifying," the seventh section of the collection, articulates the subjective reality of disabled dykes, and in so doing, it dispels myths about the quality of disabled persons' lives. "Yearning" names the process through which we politicize our realities, and hence transform them. Entitled "Reinscribing," the final section of the anthology is comprised of work which intimates the creative work that can be borne of that defiant transformation.

Finally, I have compiled, and appended to the collection, a list of resources (articles, books, videos, audiocassettes) which are relevant to disabled dykes. Although virtually every one of the anthologies noted there includes work that was produced by disabled dykes, most of those collections were edited by non-disabled dykes, or straight disabled women, who (for one reason, or another) have not indicated that such work was so produced; furthermore, although almost every one of the videos listed there focuses upon a disabled dyke(s), not all of them do, and some of them have been produced and/or directed by non-disabled women. In the instances in which a given video is accessible to Hard-of-Hearing, and Deaf, dykes, I have included this information in the blurb which describes it. In the blurb for each of the newsletters, I have indicated the various formats in which it is available.

Enjoy!

< 22 >

Notes

1. For a very provocative discussion of the ways in which 'silence,' deafness, and disablement are used in literature and everyday discourse, see Lennard J. Davis, *Enforcing Normalcy: Disability, Deafness, and the Body* (London and New York: Verso, 1995), pp. 100-126, and *passim*.

2. I put this term in quotation marks in order to indicate my disdain for the way in which it is currently used. When I lived in Vancouver in the early eighties, the term was one that we (leftists, activists, dykes) playfully directed at each other in order to remind us not to take ourselves too seriously. The way in which conservative forces have since appropriated, and redefined the term in order to maliciously use it against any and all progressive, and oppositional, movement is in fact a good example of the point that I wish to make here, namely, that language is a site of ongoing political struggle.

3. Insofar as the notions of "ability" and "disability" rely upon deeply-entrenched *ideals of normality*, I regard them as implicitly ableist and disableist ones; hence, contrary to the position which most North American activists hold, I neither use, nor endorse, the term 'able-bodied,' the phrase "with a disability," or the phrase "has a disability." However, in order to retain the integrity of each writer's work, and to affirm her right to name herself, I have not made editorial changes where these terms are used.

4. I do not draw the widely-accepted distinction between so-called "mental disability" and so-called "physical disability" for two interdependent reasons: first, that distinction relies upon a philosophically indefensible mind/body dichotomy which prevails within traditional western epistemologies, where the *mind* and the *body* are construed as two separate entities, and the rational mind controls (that is, subordinates, and gives form to) the latter construed as the irrational, chaotic body; second, the way in which the mind is venerated in western epistemologies has not only resulted in numerous hierarchies in western cultures in general (for example, the prestige, and

< 23 >

power, given to "intellectual" labour as opposed to "physical" labour) but it has also produced a hierarchy within the disability community, and movement in particular, where so-called mentally disabled persons are regarded as "naturally impaired" and so-called physically disabled persons are regarded as "socially disabled."

< 24 >

I

searching

mother/daughter
Shahnaz Stri

mother
daughter
unknown

woman sitting
wondering

a daughter
looking
for a past
searching
for history

mother
lost in
a country
walking away
not looking
perhaps wondering

daughter
lost
found
but no mother
she does not look
only thinks
of who she is

no stories
of family history
no cultural past

where are you from?

< 27 >

there are no answers
guesses
ideas

other women's stories
my own stories
my own history
made up along the way

to tell my daughter
someday

< 28 >

On Being
Shahnaz Stri

on being indian
on being south asian
on being a woman
on being an immigrant child

on what this is about
there is no family involved

i grew up amidst adults
no mothers
no fathers
no brothers
no sisters
no cousins

no relations

they are somewhere in india
lost to me here in canada

will i ever look for them

where do i start
who do i ask

a train going somewhere
in the distance

everything lost
when i came here
everything
except myself
my memories
my name

< 29 >

no papers to say my birth
where i was born
who i am
and papers to change that
papers that changed my name
changed my age
changed my citizenship

a new country
a new home
a new family

no
not a new anything

i still got lost
taking myself away from a house
with too many nightmares

still wanting to go back to india
wanting to wake up from this
pinching myself to wake up

i look for my history
read my history
ask for my history

tell my story
stitch my past
with the history
of my culture

and

here i am today

still here

< 30 >

to the bone
Sherree Clark

I've had this dream before
I'm sitting at a table
by myself
in an empty room

and laid before me in
ordered heaps
are small misshapen bones;
fingers, toes
assorted joints;
grey and yellow
hairline fissures etched
like crooked black veins

I pick one up
chew slowly
22 times for good digestion

fragments catch

in my throat and lodge
in the spaces between my teeth
few pauses exist
between the shattering of one joint
and the selection of another

I awake
before I finish
remember
that animals
when trapped
will bite off their
limbs to escape

From the series of poems entitled "Living with Arthritis."

< 31 >

spoons
Shemaya Mountain Laurel

I lie here
breakfast arrives
in another woman's hands
once again
being fed
cringing
at the word
at the reality
another woman's hands
a spoon full of food
sliding on lips
and tongue in
and out
an entire pot so many spoons
in and out
over
and over
caressing   oatmeal is the worst no
awkward sticking here corn kernels falling everywhere   oatmeal
     always
          glides

a past love and I playing sex games
with food on the interstate
how sensually can you feed the driver

no sex here, only outrage
unavoidable or starve
on my lips soft on my tongue
how do babies survive this my mouth
my center the most available entrance
to my body I
who love oral sex
this is far too strange
how can I say
I will never eat
again

< 32 >

untitled
Patrizia Tavormina

with a salivating grin in her diamond eyes
distant spirits
of remembrances invalidated by cold intrusive touches
she mutters,
"it was easier then
with a 9 millimetre in my hand
the choice
to live or die
simple"

now alive
she is paraded
with memories of foreign proddings
                            punct015 rings
                            beatings
                            sexual violations
stripped calculatingly
of faith
the choice to live or die
simple

i sit
facing her
my eyes are bloodshot
from periods when chronic pain blisters
into volcanic eruptions
breathing myself groping for ash-filled air
every moment of those thousands of seconds
i know dying would relieve me

< 33 >

i want death
like flights underneath smooth suns and flowing cotton
skies
i want death
juicy as a tender mango bite
i want death
swiftly silently
like a slicing knife

i want death
grounded a powder i can tongue suck sweetly
soothing my throat
relaxing my limbs
assuaging violent waves to ripples so soft
eyelids rest like freshly lain sheets

i want death
warm as a cool august dip

strangely enough
my choice
to die
has never been
simple

< 34 >

Mastectomy
Louise Lander

For David Sekons, M.D.

You mutilated me to save my life.
("I made a boy of you," you said with pride.)
Do I forgive you? Yes and no. My chest
is hideous, asymmetrical, and scarred.
Now cancer-free, we hope, I am in pain.
Before, malignant lump on breast, I felt
just fine, thank you. What strange disease is this
that pains with cure? And is it cure? Who knows?
More strangeness — cure is retroactive, comes
by looking back from intervals of health.
Unfair, unfair! Give me a simple plague,
with clear beginning, unambiguous end.
Instead, this wound tells me I know not what,
except I'm not the same, forever changed
to some new species with one-breasted chest
and scarred interior, groping to make sense
of such a fate; crab-cursed, but who knows why?

< 35 >

Mirror Image
Shahnaz Stri

i go around these circles
walking around myself,
looking in the mirror
and staring for hours
at the pain lined on my face,
the anger twitching my body,
the hurt hidden so well.

i can't stand to touch myself,
for fear of memories
that bring the pain.

i crouch low
trying to hide
what little of my body is left,
so the mirror can't see any longer,
so my eyes are deceived.

i go around these circles,
inside my head,
inside myself,
treading ever so softly,
hiding in the shadows
trying to disappear
ever so quietly.

but it is alerted,
i am caught in the glare
and i stare defiantly,
my anger welling up
the sadness caught in my throat,
as i clench myself not to cry.

< 36 >

i want to shout
tear apart everything in sight,
instead i look longingly
at something that is not mine
and mine,
i turn my face from the mirror,
to hide the tears from myself.

i go around these circles
and around and around,
i am always left facing myself
and trying to adjust
my sight to this body of mine,

not mine
and am no longer comfortable touching,
only striking out,
to discipline,
so that i can adjust to this sight.

< 37 >

Lost in the Swamp
Sherry Shute

"Lost in the Swamp" was written when I was sick and bed-ridden by the side effects of a spinal tap. I'd had to cancel out of a really big gig in Vancouver with the Vancouver Symphony and my life and my prospects showed only bleakness. After a couple of days, when I was finally able to sit up and play guitar, "Lost in the Swamp" came.

```
        E              G    A
Sometimes this life is like
         E           G    A
Being lost in a swamp - - - - - -

— E       G       A —

          A                    E
Going down down in the deep mud
            Bb      A    G    Gb     E
Going down down down down down

          E              G        A
Shadow jungle's thick and tall
      E                 G      A
Rain and pain and fear is all

— E       G       A —


          A
No   sunlight
                      E
Can't find your way
                    Bb    A    G    Gb
Can't find your way - ay - ay - ay

— E       G       A —


   D
Ooh -ooh-ooh
   A
Lost in the swamp
   D
Ooh -ooh-ooh
   G           A
Lost in the swamp
```

< 38 >

—E   G   A—

     E   G A
If the shade gators don't get you

   E   G   A
Shadow fear will

—E   G   A—

 A
Afraid to hide in the dark

               E G A
You can't see to run - - - - - - - -

Bb   A G Gb
Run - un - un - un

GUITAR CHORDS

number on the left side indicates fret number

O indicates open string

< 39 >

the hand that grasps
Sherree Clark

the hand that grasps mine is
large and firm;
my hand
bony and motionless
frail and useless as a broken wing
is easily crushed in
introduction

I have a painting above
my bed of a woman
who has luminescent flowers for hair;
she smiles,
her face wan and
full of mystery,
she has hands that come out of her neck
and out of one ear
three hands as slender as winter birches
fingers crooked and
spidery

she knows about being
Prometheus bound
I wonder how she looks so calm
while offering up those hands

< 40 >

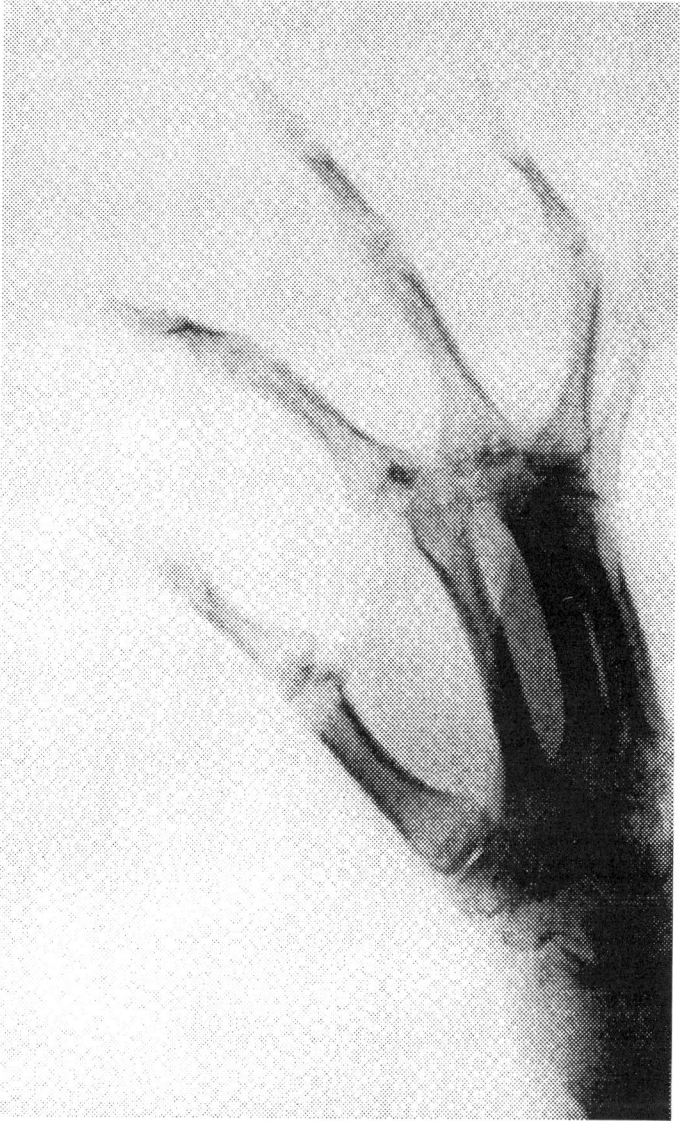

From the series of poems entitled "Living with Arthritis."

< 41 >

II

becoming

untitled

Patrizia Tavormina

I am waking up
to the rhythms of Audre Lorde's words
resonating around my forehead
wrapped
like the bandanna with a copper penny inside
you used to heal
my first bee sting
underneath a shiftless Sicilian sun and prowling midday air
on tilled red soil
i am coated
by the glossy unperforated surface
of a honey apple

i never understood your words
which come to me now
open
like a waterfall
once contained behind a towering dam
released
they blast forth
almost too fast for me to sip
now i am rarely thirsty

it was that attitude
i grew up with
like a thick heavy iron
between my shoulders
the "yes boss" disposition
you showed to most
holding together a mural of perfection
impeccably impenetrable
so no one could fault you

< 45 >

except yourself
the one you couldn't run from
although you tried through 5 children
who unashamed
display their faults like hard-earned badges
you thought we never learnt "malafigura"[1]
only we did learn
too hard
feigned appearances to benefit a status quo
we did not necessarily want to support

bowing to upper-class relatives
        employers
        fathers
        sons
even an ex-husband
you first feministly kicked out
then later
let your regret
burn scars into the faces of female relatives
by encouraging them
to stay chained in abusive marriages
        out of guilt
        out of malafigura
        out of omertà — the code of silence

i did not want to inherit
you servitude
i wanted your anger
your telling your husband/our father
to FUCK OFF without apologies
telling your boss to fuck off
as he harassed
faster, Bitch, faster
even machines have limits
but you rarely were

< 46 >

angry

just worked endlessly
like a martyr
i carry your sacrifices
imbedded into me
like thick rusty nails
it is hard to move
sometimes

your elder daughter
inherited your authority
she only functions under stress
craves success
like a drug she has never tried before
delirious

SHE learned to say fuck off
to keep her rage
on the tip of her tongue
where it could be viewed
with each genuine smile

i'm twenty-seven
you are sixty
and as you are
about to become
thrice the grandmother matriarch
i
wonder about living
give myself three more years
sometimes one
sometimes six months
i never wanted life
only one of my own
that never came

< 47 >

i watch time swipe past me
as you delve fast into
a busy retirement

i used to feel i was forty
now
i feel like i'm twenty-two — yet to make choices
i become
one of your facial creases
grooved deeper
with each extended yawn

zii^2 say we look alike
i am your splitting image
i was always suspect of that
given your bleached blonde hair ever since I can remember
only recently in the family picture
my hair gelled back
i saw your lips
in mine
your eyebrows and forehead

our hands are not alike
mine are long and thin
nor are we the same height
i am tall
people say i have piano hands
and a dancer's stride
skills i wanted to learn
lessons you could not afford to offer

i used to say
i got my strength from you
but i am not so sure anymore
that you fought in ways
that gave me room to breathe

< 48 >

i have schooling
way beyond what you
could have ever hoped
for me
for yourself
but due to a disability
i may never earn a weekly income
like you did
may never work a day
like you do
never own property
or start a family
but like you
i may hate every
waking day
i did not ask for
so we are
reflections in a stream

that stay still
no matter how fast
the waves push forward
or backward

i know you tried
to save me
but i had left you
way before i was born
which i say
without bitterness or sadness
but with the certainty
of the frown you wear
each time we tread
a cultural faux-pas and you wonder
time and time again
with a roll of your movie-screen eyes
and a look that travels ancestors back
who bore these Canadian children?

< 49 >

i have become a statistic
on the welfare roles
the people i used to fight for;
theories then so convenient
now useless
as i fight
to struggle the dawn of each day

like Frida Kahlo
i watch the world
beneath beastly eyebrows
i might also leave myself
behind

i wait and wonder
mother
will you go before i do
because i could not bear
to have you live/swallow
the pain of my death
which will come
as sure as the laugh lines
just forming at the edge
of our dark chestnut eyes

We have always seen
through each other
so even death
may not come as a surprise to you
who has been myself
in another lifetime
on another land
where you died from a weak heart
i could not revive you

< 50 >

through centuries together
i know your every motion
your worries
your dreams

but back alley moons and cat screams
don't wake me
running to your bed
at 1 a.m. anymore
your church pew voice has long since
ceased hollering our names
at the end of a long summer girl's day
i only cross those trafficked bridges
that have pedestrian paths
and i know
copper pennies in cloth wraps
don't heal
bee stings

1. Malafigura: a grave stigma attached to Sicilians who break the
code of Sicilian-sanctioned social and moral behaviour.
2. Zii: aunts

< 51 >

the good mother
Shahnaz Stri

she always sought my approval
with a hug
a smile
or a kiss on the forehead.

she would point out
what a good mother
she was.

a good mother
for these
five
six
seven
unwanted children.

a good mother
for us.

ignoring the facts
of our lives...

locking doors
a leather belt
a cage inside a house.

i know what she wanted...
my approval
my gratefulness
yet she ignored
these simple facts.

< 52 >

the pain from her smile
the hurt from her love
and she ignored them,
like she sought approval.

she was a lonely woman
i think.
but the facts
can never be
forgotten.

< 53 >

Green Beans and the Blue Angel
an excerpt
magie dominic

Green Beans and the Blue Angel *is a manuscript in progress, based on the autobiographical poem "notes from the cover," published in* ARC *magazine in Ottawa, 1994. Violence has been a part of my life for as long as I can remember and it is my experiences with violence that I'm attempting to articulate and the miracle of escaping the madness. "Betrayal" is an excerpt from part one of the book.*

Betrayal

I watch clouds swimming by, changing form, slowly and tenderly kissing. The sky finds room for all of them. There is never a cloud without a sky. They all belong and there's room for more. I place my own cloud there and watch it dissolve into a thousand different layers. The trees look up in amazement. They had no idea I was so complex. Only the sky knew and made room without question. Everything changes form before the eyes of those who are looking up. Everything is complex. The sky makes room gladly as seasons change below.

The light seems to change as well. It's the way it falls on things. Whole areas of trees are exposed. Parts of buildings become visible. Leaves fall and dark brown limbs jut into space, weightless except for the light. More birds are visible in the fall. Or maybe it just seems that way because of the falling leaves and the light.

No matter where you are in the autumn, leaves fall, and things that were once concealed are now exposed.

In the summer, with the woods fat with foliage, the light is locked out. It was like this on the highways I remember in Newfoundland.

It was like this at the cabin.

The cabin is difficult to capture. In winter it was pictur-

< 54 >

esque, buried and cold. In summer it was alive with nature, isolation, and darkness.

You had to walk up a little hill to a field to get real sunlight. The field was completely untouched. Down below on the unpaved road, you'd never suspect this field even existed. But it did. A magical meadow in the middle of the woods. I went there to get warm in tall stalks of golden grass.

Is gold spun from straw or is straw spun from gold?

The field was bordered on all sides by trees. Thick clusters of spruce and birch and maple. Some of them misshapen and odd-looking because of the hard winters. But they were majestic in the sunlight even with their crooked backs and twisted limbs.

If you were in the field picking strawberries and the timing was just right, you could lift up the green leaves and the touch of your fingers would make the berry fall off its stem, right into your hand. Some of the berries needed to be pulled. They didn't give up the field easily. The white ones were to be left to mature. The ones that fell into my hand were my favourite. There was no struggle involved.

The embrace of light was everywhere and it was quiet as only light can be. It gave each leaf an identity. Rather, it confirmed the identity. Within minutes, everything would change. The light over everything was blue, like a thin cloak, like picasso's blue period and one long streak of cloud would stretch across the sky like a highway. I wanted to walk on it. To take it to wherever it was leading. I would be its humble traveller, quietly stepping on the softness, staying within the boundaries of cloud road.

Light danced around a row of white cotton nightgowns hanging on a line, outside a convent in France.

I didn't see this but I know it happened.

It made the gowns move gently, like the women who wore them. The light made the creme satin ribbons around the neck glisten like fine jewelry. It surrounded these garments worn in sleep, filled them with the light of light. It

< 55 >

had been doing this for centuries, as long as convents have existed. And clothes lines.

The white gowns were like holy skins of angels hung out to dry. There was everything peaceful about this image. There was no violence involved. It wasn't like rabbit skins hung to dry, violence pinning them in place as accurately as gunshot. These white gowns were like the quiet skins of angels, like teardrops gently moving and filled with light.

Down by the cabin there was darkness.

There were two different highways and two different grandfathers. One was from the really old country, a shop-keeper, a man who eventually became an invalid with a hip that wouldn't heal and spent his last months confined to a tiny dark room in a huge house that was otherwise sun-filled. I don't know his past. He always wanted water to wash his hands. It was like a ritual to him, or maybe it seemed that way to me. It seemed religious. I can't explain it now. I couldn't understand it then. This was my father's father. I would get him a fresh pan of water when we went to visit in this tiny town. Botwood. I don't think it was even big enough to call a town, whatever it is that you call places before they become towns. Hamlets. He'd pray in his tiny dark room and wash his hands, with light everywhere else in the house except near him, as if he were being forced to die before his time. Light deprivation.

Then there was the other grandfather. The one I want to forget but can't. The man with the large hands for chopping wood, splitting logs and splitting other things open too. This is his story. This is not a fairy tale.

It had to do with a lake. Driving there on summer sundays. When our car reached the place on the highway where the house was, down at the bottom of a large cow pasture, everyone would leave except for my grandfather and me. My age doesn't matter. I was young. Eight or nine. Maybe seven. My grandfather said his leg was "bad." So my parents decided that I was to stay in the car to keep him company. This is

< 56 >

what I was to do on sunday afternoons. To be quiet and to keep him company.

The front seat of the car was silent. We sat next to one another, him on the passenger side, me in the middle part. I think the seat was covered with plastic, washable.

Around us, on the outside of the windows, were hundreds of trees. Nothing but spruce and birch and maple. I don't remember hearing birds sing. They may have been there but I don't remember them. The highway at that time was unpaved and when an occasional car would whiz by, a cloud of brown dust settled on the windows like curtains. This grandfather had a glass eye and sometimes he'd remove it while he and I were alone and place it on the dashboard. An eye staring back at me. At the two of us. And I was told to be quiet. Not to tell anyone about anything. Amidst this solitude of spruce and birch and maple this grandfather would begin to remove my clothing and put his hands inside me, silently looking straight ahead, except for the eyeball resting on the dashboard. I looked straight ahead too, through the dirty car window, up to the sky.

The car radio was never on. Total silence.

There is a lot more to this story but I don't know if I'm able to write it. The pen I need is red like a cinder that's been smouldering for almost half a century. It wants to write about the evil of this man. His hands doing things they never should have done. It wants to write about the feelings of total child abandonment, beginning with saturday nights, knowing sunday was next and the car ride up there and knowing what was to come and asking if I could go down to the house with everyone else but being refused. This happened several times. Everything happened several times. Everything was silent. Windows rolled up tight. Needing to go to the bathroom and being taken out of the car, across the unpaved highway. Not being allowed to go down to the house. Being taken up an embankment and into a woodsy part of the forest. I remember the birch trees. There I would squat,

< 57 >

sunday dress up around my shoulders, while he stood behind me, staring at me in that position, and he picked leaves for me to wipe myself. He'd stare at me for a long time before handing me a leaf, the forest now rubbing against the hurting parts of my child body. Then we'd silently return to the car and just stare ahead, through the dusty windshield. At least this is what I did. I didn't look at him, both eyes inside his head by now. I just stared ahead. I've always wondered why, in all those sundays that summer, never once did anyone ever come up from the big house to see if I wanted anything. A sandwich or even a glass of water.

The cabin is where the nightmares began. My bedroom. Next to the unfurnished back room with hard backed beetles falling to the floor. They made sounds like ball point pens falling, several ball point pens in the middle of the night.

I would dream of being captured by strangers who were always on horseback outside the back room. I'd run to the front door in these dreams, like silent movies. Even my dreams were silent. I would run through the cabin to the front but there'd be more strangers, tall, on horseback, waiting.

This was to become a recurring nightmare all through the years we lived up the highway. That's what being away from the city meant. Up the highway. It was never indicated how far up. It was as if you'd disappeared. You were now "up the highway," like "laid to rest" or "overseas."

Something that broad and vague.

I would wake up hard, like something had slapped me and I'd wake up crying and sometimes, if my father was home, he'd come in from the other bedroom with a flashlight or a kerosene lamp and sit with me.

In the autumn on the way to school I'd pray for the car to crash. An accident, taking me. I couldn't stand any more humiliation, any more hands inside me. Better for the damn car to crash. I was ready to die. How long does a person have to live anyway?

< 58 >

Crash car. Crash. Dear sweet Jesus, please make the car crash.

I tried to get away from the little girl sitting on the front seat of the car, looking through the dusty window. I tried to get away from the little girl sitting silent, staring straight ahead, with the old man next to her, looking wherever he was looking. I tried to get away from the little girl in that car, sitting abandoned, betrayed, isolated, her lower body parts aching.

I tried to get away from her all of my life but it was useless. Her large eyes would be forever staring back at me through so many afternoons as I sat there in silence, trying to see the sky, listening for the people who never came, trying to figure out what I had done, who I had done it to, when I had done it. What was it that I had done in this short life to cause me to be in this situation. I tried to get away from it, to run from it in my mind, but her eyes would stare back at me for the rest of my life. And the eyes (her eyes) were haunting and unrelenting.

There is a stillness that exists sometimes around five a.m., a peace that has settled on buildings and trees during the night. And the further you get away from the city, the longer it seems this calm lasts, until, if you get far enough away from the noises of civilization, the stillness lingers on the trees and on the ground from sunrise to sunrise, from season to season.

This calmness didn't exist on the trees near the car where my grandfather sat. Where I sat next to him.

NO!

He was sitting next to me. I was NEVER sitting next to him.

This stillness and peace didn't exist on the trees there. In this part of the Canadian forest the trees were screaming. They made loud piercing sounds. They doubled over in pain. They threw up. They held on to each other in fear and disbelief. They pulled themselves up from their roots, throw-

< 59 >

ing up as they ran. And the smell of their vomit permeated
the forest.

A family that permits child abuse is a suicidal family.

< 60 >

Body Shield
Allison Sletcher

ink on paper, 12" w x 9" h

The design "Body Shield" fits over the heart and under the breasts as a tattoo. The images used from Celtic Legend are:

Sea Serpents:	guardians of the unconscious
Snakes/serpents:	the unconscious
Birds:	spirit, freedom
Fish:	wisdom, knowledge of spiritual, ovaries
Water:	the unconscious, spiritual world, domain of woman and matriarchy
Ninth wave:	spiritual world, otherworld

< 61 >

III

loving

Love Isn't
Pat Parker

I wish I could be
the lover you want
come joyful
bear brightness
like summer sun

Instead
I come cloudy
bring pregnant women
with no money
bring angry comrades
with no shelter

I wish I could take you
run over beaches
lay you in sand
and make love to you

Instead
I come rage
bring city streets
with wine and blood
bring cops and guns
with dead bodies and prison

I wish I could take you
travel to new lives
kiss niños on tourist buses
sip tequila at sunrise

Instead
I come sad
bring lesbians

< 65 >

without lovers
bring sick folk
without doctors
bring children
without families

I wish I could be
your warmth
your blanket

All I can give
is my love.

I care for you
I care for our world
if I stop
caring about one
it would be only
a matter of time
before I stop
loving
the other.

< 66 >

Her Gift To Me Is A Window
Laura Hershey

This rooted
rounded house I have built   my life
odd angles and ghosts
painted walls   strong supports
room histories   favorite books
this structure has served
for one
through years' discovery
has weathered squalls
held up by sound structure
protected by kindly neighbors

Now into this life moves another
carrying her own
blueprints   wielding tools   cans of paint

She rearranges
my furniture,
stirs my surprised spirit   she cuts
through walls
exposing views on pain and beauty

Her gift to me is a window
on blossoming joy   gardens we together
tend   growing
precious shoots vulnerable
to crows
              and winds painting   new histories
              we make up as we
                                  go along

We go along framing
with what little   we know
and all   we feel   this vision

< 67 >

She gives me love
and her gift to me is a window
        letting in
        all I
        was never offered   and with it
desire
need
fear   of losing

She gives me attention
and her gift to me is a window
        thrown   suddenly open
        to a self   startled
        by spotlight
I try to close my eyes

She gives me my body
and her gift to me is a window
        on mountains of pleasure   playing   riotous
        the fullness of a smile   stretching legs wide
and on
        the power of my invisible blue
        energy
and on
        violent assaults arising
        from a weak cough
        haunting weariness
        angry hurts
        my harsh mind tells me
        I should know how to stop
        but can't

She gives acceptance
and her gift to me is a window
        on starcradled wholeness   as my rough facets join
        in sacred crystal   and begin to allow
        a passage of light

< 68 >

and on

      rejection
      my young
      and old pain
      all the years my open door
      was passed by   again and again

The gusts that enter
the moths and flies
frighten a lonely occupant

the heat
    chill
    panicked misguided birds
    dust
    rains
    scenes
threaten an untried house   until

the touch of her hand
brings back   sun   and   gentle breezes

And her gift to me is a window

< 69 >

full day
Margot K. Louis

though I can't walk a block, we spent nine hours
one day in bed (with a short break for lunch)
kissing with soft exploratory lips
the cheek, edge of the lip,
the open salty nostril, downy neck,
the ear's whorled hollow storm of erotic lightnings
that burst in yellow all over the loins
(I sucked your lobe once; when you could speak again,
you asked me not to),
getting each other's hair in our mouths and giggling about it,
the roof of the mouth (what a kindly provision,
to have skin on the inside of our bodies
as well as all over us on the outside),
the nubbly silky inside of the cheek,
the flexible stubborn muscle inside
(do you remember how we struggled
whose tongue would get inside whose teeth,
tongue-wrestlers, both too butch for stability),
your strong square dimpled chin, my pointed chin
and down the curd and curve and softness of our necks
to where our nipples kissed, our bellies slid in
sweat, salt-sweet, and for hours we suckled
licked the hard round of the nipple-tip,
or slowly into living wonder wet mouths woke
each breast, kissed, laved, until my breasts pulled me toward you
and close, closer still, till our skins breathed each other
and our cunts slid together, astonishing
each other with our wetness, feeling
a glisten, a slithering, our glisten and slither
and you delicately said *may I?* and then
kissed in surprise
we felt each hair and each
lip and each lip kissed you back and

< 70 >

we came into sleep and we came awake
and started from the other end
and you couldn't understand why
I wasn't tired. I wasn't tired at all.
why, when my whole skin breathed and fed from yours
would I tire? why when the sun shone in every cell
sacred in my flesh would I be chilled?

< 71 >

"...and I will have sex again"
Daphne L. Hill

It's our first date. We're sitting in my car. "Uh, can I ask you a personal question," she hesitates, glances at me and then averts her eyes. I know it's *the question.* "Yes, well it depends," I say, enjoying her discomfort. I wonder if she's ready for my answer. I'm always taken aback when they ask, although I've come to expect it from the dates I will not see again. The women who see the me beyond my crippled mask of metal need not ask; they know I have sex.

And I will have sex again.

She fed me a burrito only hours after my surgery. She, we, knew I would have sex again. She fed me slowly, the fork sliding in and out of my mouth. Our eyes sparkled with joy and desire. We both secretly prayed that my paralysis wouldn't extend up to my nipples. Please, oh please, don't let me lose them too. I lay in intensive care with breast-touch on my mind. My heart is beating 122 beats per minute for days. I teeter on the edge of survival and still I wonder if my breasts will ever feel her touch again. I want to reach back in time and comfort us both with knowing that I feel. Nipples, ears, neck, arms, fingers, mouth, armpits, shoulder and big broad spacious back.

And now, my lovers learn about touch. Some cannot hear; they speak back with a roughness that is numbing. Others know the language of feel and touch so gentle, it rides like waves over skin, ears, and neck.

I ask myself why can't I remember what a good fuck feels like. If only I'd known then in my plunging of grief that this body wants more than the in-in deep thick feel of fingers. My rage reaches back to millions of touches ago. I am shut down and tired of conjuring up memories, feelings of deep familiar caverns. She thought she knew just the right spot. "Do you? Do you, now? Anything?" I lay, tears streaming down my cheeks, ashamed of my inadequacy and blankness of memory before the line at my chest rendered me sexless.

< 72 >

Change.

I went to the theatre. There I watched a love scene between two women. French poetry and lace, endless love-making. The tingle deep in my chest caught me looking around, had my friends noticed my lust? The rush of desire, the hot liquid feeling that brings wetness to thighs, and then higher, caught me by surprise. Caught me wishing, feeling hopeful. I began to reach back and feel the dripping onto clitoris and labia. I knew I would have sex again.

I wrote her, "Where have you been; I'm out of the hospital. Come home." There she is, knocking, writing, responding. I must come. How do I come? Help me, make me, love me. Beautiful she, are you here? Wake up. I need you. No tears don't cry sweet beautiful she. Wipe them away and learn with me. My rage stops me; I sit on the edge of ecstasy. Our kissing brings tingling in to linger between my breasts, deep into my root. Feeling — head, follicle, tingle, pulsing. I get goose bumps, like listening to a good blues tune. You play me. Honey, a good fuck will give my head and my body a life you may only know through my words, moans and sighing delight in our calm after.

Listen please. I remember lamenting to friends that I felt not like a woman, not like a man and not like anything at all. Where is my cunt; I've lost it. Now I only pee from the hole nature made and roughly took away. Where is my sex? My womanliness feels blank. I sit in the theatre, I singe with desire. Damn, how do I capture this? Please do something to let me come to you once again rocking hips and sway into your arms.

Oh God. I need the coming, not the grief again. We lock eyes and tears stream down. My desire is so very strong for you, beautiful dark-haired she. We used to have it so easy.

Now. Will you harness me and just please make it happen once again. How, oh how, do you do that? The books explain it with such sterility. Yes, you can still have sex; you can reproduce. What's sexual about having babies? I have abso-lutely no interest in birthing babies. I want an orgasm. Your essays insult me. My memory races back to age eleven. I am

< 73 >

on my bed discovering my clitoris, rubbing it until my hand ached and my bed shook. I was good to me then, not like now. My only good is in my grieving this loss I cannot reckon with. I tell my therapist I must have a lover. I need to come. She suggests a vibrator. I say "what? I can't feel remember?" Speechless, she utters, "nipples?" Oh yea, fun. Alone. Maybe a feather on my skin, my hand on my head.

Call out, touch me like she used to. I need some practice.

I will have sex again. Here is what I want to say to you who do not know and may not care. Someday, like me, you may not feel; you may be numb and grieving. Be prepared. I want you to line up at my door, waiting for my expertise. I want to be an expert. I am an expert. Let me erase your fear.

I woke up last night. I touched my arm. It felt electric and like I might enjoy more touching. I did it again and more, yet again and more. I turned out my light and removed my shirt. I wanted to come. I could feel it. The possibility lay lurking beneath my skin and behind my neck like my lover's hand. I touched all over my feeling skin, light brushes on my nipples and down around my arms, up elbows and turning to my hairline. I was scared to life and turned over to quiet my arousal. Asleep, my desire dreamt of the day when my hand can do what only a lover has done or undone. I am shaken. I am grieving. I will have sex again.

Ah there. Oh please. Oh yes ahhh... Touch me there, right up my neck, ear, now my crown. Please, oh yes. My first lesbian told me I needed a man inside me. She liked penetration too. She's married now. Guess she took her own advice. Me? I know the only reason I liked it so much was because the she inside me was fingers and I like only that. Touch me there; enter and yes I'm curled in the crest of your palm and tongue. I could not dare imagine my lazy afternoons of coming to Ferron and Janis stripped away; flat, slip, fall and severed.

Lying in bed while in intensive care. Nurses unknowingly pity us. They smile down on you, me. Fear reeks through their words, "how are you, Hon?" "Fine, uh, could I have

< 74 >

another shot?" "It hurts again." My back lay broken, my spirit dangled at each end of the severed cord. She walks in. My doctor? Brown eyes surge down into mine and she winks. There is no pity in her eyes, only healing and concern. She tries to know; she cares and she is stunning. I've died and gone to gorgeous doctor heaven. My clitoris sends heat up to my chest like balls of fire; they melt slowly and spread into my ribcage. I remember to breathe or catch my breath. Stop, you must stop. She'll feel you, see you, and want you.

I know I will have sex again. The mystery grieves me; the wonder and painful thought of loss becomes me. There she was, looking into me. A single tear rolls from her eye. Silently, she cries. Oh how I fall in love with her painful cry. It lies still and heavy inside of her, slowly it pours. She could cry for a thousand scenes with one silent tear. She kisses my forehead, eyes, cheeks, and a sweet wet kiss on my lips. I am enraged at her assumption. How the hell could you want me? Flaccid and lifeless, my belly round, my legs thin and unmoving. I am unresponsive and loose. I refuse to touch my body below the waist, can't stand the touch of skin that is numb, skin that used to tingle, right there. Tubes come out of my vagina, my nose, my lung, and god if only a tube was in my chest pumping out this lust I wish I could deny.

I am weeping as I write, how lost I was and still can be. The pain of yesterday is very recent despite the distance in years. When pleasure visits me now it is with sweet relief that I greet it.

My life is full of sex. I can't imagine ever wondering. I can't fathom not having. I find erotic pleasure in the ordinary. I see the sensuous nature of my world in easy moments. I go to the ballet. I watch plays and I sit still for hummingbirds. These are the sexual. Gazing at a woman's neck, listening to music, eating pesto and rich ice cream. I have come to know orgasm through my lover's eyes and hearing the wood floors creak under a dancers feet. I experience sex in the touch, breast, rage and her liquid coming.

She and I had our time, our raging and our swirling rush, feel passion. She rubbed her body on mine. Her breasts met

< 75 >

mine and we rocked in motion to our pulsing beats of life. Feeling her sweat emerge under my hands was enough to bring my body forth as if liquid were rising up out of my vagina. Kissing her was like kissing labia and orgasm with each lip touch. I knew I had found my sex again.

She knew my rage and my coming way as well. I exploded into silence and a turned back. Cold wall, stare and pout at her ineptness. Damn you, make me come. We spent hours not talking. We slammed doors with our eyes that had only moments before led us into a rich soulful expanse. Suddenly with one fall of body, she was no longer timid she felt safe. Once she coiled inward at my touch and now she raged at the absence of my pressured hand upon her glistening lips. We remarked at the irony of our flip. I, left numb and motionless in response to her touch, she now writhing and impatient with my grief. Each time she entered me, my eyes closed. Remember, relax, visualize. Damn. There are hundreds upon thousands of orgasms resting in my mind. Make them real all over again. She, not one to take responsibility for my pain pulled me on top of her asking for, demanding. "If not you, dear one, then me." Each time she came the concrete in my chest hardened. I was so resentful at her joy. I will have sex again.

Now I have found a way to my heart, my center and my passion. I come like the rushing sea. I waited three, five, six and now eight years and the sex is heavier, wetter and more sky-lifting, more body-plunging deepness into soul-filling ecstasy. I come into arms of pulse and touch, tender, tingle, soft light touch on skin, hair and lips. I cannot get enough. I teach without pause and breathe with bodies that dare to step off into deepness with me. She traces a trail on my arm which reaches right to my core, shaking my head and my loins. My orgasms are complete only when I'm too tired to let the feeling reel onward. I scream and that completes my exploding self. I scream of liberation. I scream of joy and I purge the grief that never visits. It sits like dust in my lungs, expelled each glorious time. My now is solid rapture. I am having sex again.

< 76 >

Love Pain and the Fading of Orchids

Anne-Marie Alonzo

I

to hold seek   remembrance   and to show heart not
knowing why or what it might confuse   holding as in a
desert where you   mostly I   await night and day and night
to pass without wind nor sand cries mostly and sighs as to
say thighs thinking of yours hoping for whispers in stride
forgetting time absorbing it gently and you say: truce! ask for
some while I vanish while I do.

II

please don't leave me but if   and you might   I'll shiver
and die I'll certainly not live for I find my breath in you
only there   and the mist covers the orchids from your body
so overwhelming in the light   you choose candles light a
fire as I beg to see you and in you where pearls lay   my
hand vaguely my lips tongue and hand   somewhere the
cry   do you say pleasure or should I when tears submerge
you (or I! do we know)   I   let me repeat myself I do love
you   infinitely there are no more words as I search for you
find you lose you please don't leave me not yet not as the
candles are still melting your heart pounding against yours
my body all around there is my face mouth tongue lips nose
eyes   there is   and the unique scent of you on my neck
I was there hurt there you healed me   warmth runs thru
me we are   you I as I you   you'll disappear I'll stop
breathing will breathe no air that smells of saffron and spice.

III

somewhere   the cities have changed resemble each other
as I search for your eyes your lips so dark like some parts
of you I wait say nothing wait silently or cry nobody hears
or listens it is you and I   the distance unbearable the miles

< 77 >

and days nothing to approach you when you ask for peace
and to be left   alone   you forget try desperately to leave
me! the words are hidden and your eyes how can I   not
knowing seeing you   agree say yes to the pain accepting
death wanting it all costs without you life is life nothing else
so much less   but I stop do not speak lay in bed tears are
scarce the heart has died every day night and day   while
you stay silent.

IV

silver and gold around my neck never to be taken off then
you'd leave I'd die or be terribly sick for the loss of you
the chain is off (you've left me) put back on begging you to
stay   within   caress embrace kiss gently as if you   and
not I   had the power to survive the leaves have been
stricken by gold   you were the jeweller I the poet what
have we saved.

V

chasing you away keeping you the swords have crumbled
please allow me to scream no sorrow should be kept silent
no sadness so intense my tongue refuses to talk every
whisper! as for her standing there closer than life begging
holding me to stay! not leave (for or because of you)   tears
this time   hers   her eyes wanting she pleads says please
as I leave her and you   I renounce   what is there she
says   me   kissing my eyes lips and tongue grasping it
what is there if not the scent of you always within the eyes
of you the dark ships to follow distance fades the trees linger
as I do never to call you   again.

VI

the strength the trees I look up to my legs arms grasping
you're impossible to find   running and you know I don't
refuse to   the body is yours mine has been dead do you
prefer asleep!   to awaken only by your touch feeling as if
nothing has happened I have walked with you played
jumped dove never fear nor pain clinging to your eyes dark

< 78 >

as nights of love and lust never ending eyes prolonged by
khol fine lines of laughter your neck resembles your mouth
so soft under my tongue impeccable as I watch remember
your picture has gone I can't won't look at you pray not to
forget the features fading or is it the memory so terribly soon
I love you   that has been said thought desperately believed
in where are you at three o'clock this sunday afternoon.

VII

I hate   you not being here my body has gone astray is not
reacting the hurt pain my hands bleed cut my fingers seek
you're the phone your lips thighs hold me   I   have nothing
left lay in bed sick (some say because you're leaving!)   and
I desert the body do not care to live your breasts forget me
I never them   do you still remember the nights mornings
the hours never ending the light licking your back and mine
who are or are we   other than ourselves torn as you chose
and choose again without me saying yes or die in peace.

VIII

look   open your legs to hear feel the aching from one to
one side of the bed you buy a car to come to me for a day
hour minute to share never more you are taken as you know
and she takes all never lets you out of grip sight   she says
love without blinking says hate when speaking of me in
terms always certain grinning can't stand as you say no and
manipulates you and refuses to see hear you burst in anger
order me to stop as I stop naturally you love her what else
is there to say.

IX

months pass you go come go again there's no end to your
travels and always as far from me as possible you call write
say love words as songs as I wait once again   not knowing
you have left me will leave and leave the pain is too strong
brutal your eyes you cry for the loss of her I for yours afar
we become estranged so much away from each other   you

< 79 >

don't love me you say not in the same way you say that as
truth while I fall to the ground.

X

I don't see the phone keeps ringing my eyes are dead to the
world   I have not found a dying way your picture is
watching over me you are the jeweller mold me I won't say
take me back will not speak words of love nor beg as you
propose friendship I won't hear need your thighs around my
waist need your scent to breathe   I love you   not moving
while my body aches moans from the definite loss of you.

< 80 >

liberation
Margot K. Louis

my lover said,
    she spent her life
     taking care
(raped and beaten) of her raped and beaten
      sisters
        and brothers,
     of her husband (locked tight in his fears)
     of her daughters.

my lover said to me
    to push your wheelchair,
    shop for you, make your meals,
    is just the same
    old trap.

she fell in love
    not with me, but with the old
      trap.

as I discovered
the honour of touching her
    in every finger-touch and kiss,

she learned to think
    better
  of herself
to expect
    better
  than a trap.

she's on the move.

she's off.

she's gone.

< 81 >

IV

positioning

To My Other Bodies
Connie Panzarino

It's strange
this relationship,
   -relationships.
You are each my hands, my feet,
   sometimes my eyes, and mouth to interpret clearer
speech.

There have been so many of you in my life
   I lose count.
Can't remember
   your name
   the face.
I see you years later
   in a crowd
   at the beach,
and Body says, "I know you well,"
while Mind shouts, "No! I don't remember.
Not-a-lover-not-a-friend, but *who?*"

I spend more time with you than with my lover.
Our boundaries blur with painful necessity
      as I know when you are hungry, but saying you're not,
      or constipated, or doubting yourself,
and you suffer my medical abuses as if they were your own,
Just as you know my everything
      from my love of chocolate, my bank balance, and what
brand of tuna I buy
      to how my twisted body must be placed at night so
that we both get a good night's sleep,
and how I need you to wash my labia
      my hair
      my teeth

< 85 >

but need you to be invisible,
so I can feel alone
        at dinner with my lover while you feed me;
invincible,
so you never get sick and
get me sick,

and always on time for your work shift.

I pay you, but it's never enough to compete with
        Burger King,
        or McDonalds,
but it's all I have.
It's all THEY will give
        a person with a disability to pay a personal assistant.

Why do you do it?
        I know your friends think this job is weird.
        People at Woolworth's think you're all my daughters,
as a way to rationalize your attentiveness to my every move,
        or normalize the closeness they see between us

you personal assistants are a crazy bunch
        with precious humour and the insight to know
that crips are far more interesting than Big Macs,
and that sometimes
        we must cross a boundary or risk climbing over a fence
to realize our fullest sense of self
as it is reflected in those around us.

< 86 >

Thursday Afternoon and the Laws of the Universe
zana

you probably won't want to hear some of this, kristie, and i probably won't tell you. but, for my own sake, I need to write it down somewhere.

the funny thing is that i can't tell you a lot of the good stuff, either, because you'd make more of it than is really there. for instance, there was that day in march, not long after we arrived here. sanda had pointed out the asparagus bed that needed weeding, and you and i sat there for a timeless lovely time, talking a little, pulling out weeds and heaping them in a pile, breathing in the flowery country air. i can still feel the spring sun gentle on my skin and hear your leisurely laughter. you knew the names of the prettiest wildflowers and i knew the weeds that were good for food and medicine. for me, those are soft memories.

i really wish i could feel the way you feel about me. i don't let you know how hard i try — it isn't very flattering, is it, when someone has to try? i've agonized over it with my sister and with my co-counsellor; they both say that if you don't feel it, you just don't. it's okay. but i still ask myself why i'm not attracted to you. is it just a physical thing? you're so little and thin and blond and there's a vague sourish smell about you. maybe it's because you laugh at simple things and ask me to explain my subtler jokes. sometimes it seems that everything you do irritates me. i know i pick on you if you lie on my bed with your shoes on or if you slam my car door with the seatbelt hanging out. when other wimin do the same things, i let it go by.

i have to be grateful to you but it doesn't make me love you. in fact, i wonder if it doesn't kill love a little? you are so faithful to me, always listen to my problems, always bring me back a treat from town. certainly, you've made it possible for me to live here at all. i never would have asked these wimin, whom i hardly knew, to welcome me into their midst

< 87 >

and split firewood for me, and help me with my laundry, and all the zillion unexpected things that come up. although it's supposed to be a work exchange, the fact is that i don't cook much for you anymore; it's too impractical, we eat so differently. yet you continue to do what i need done.

the *real* energy exchange has come to be my counselling. have you noticed that i rarely bring my deeper thoughts to you anymore? actually, i have fewer problems than i did when we first got here. there you were: running around with the other non-disabled wimin, learning to use a chain saw and put up fence posts. i couldn't see where the hell i fit in.

now i feel more solid here. i have strong relationships with both naomi and sanda, as well as with you. in fact, i've become very fond of each of them — i think you wouldn't be pleased to know just *how* fond. i feel quite happy here. going to creek's place has given me a chance to get to know the wimin on her land; co-counselling with her once a week, i let off any steam that builds up.

you, on the other hand, have no confidante but me, and your list of dissatisfactions keeps growing. like when you came over the other night. kristie, i was really annoyed at you because it was so late. but being as i was brought up to be, so cursedly tactful and polite, i comforted you. you probably didn't even notice how i felt. i held you and your tears fell on me and i actually felt *repelled* — i wanted to go back to the drawings i had been doing, with only the sounds of crickets instead of your choking sobs.

and when your complaints are about naomi or sanda, i feel pulled in half. i try to patch things up, to get you to understand them, and them to understand you, but it drains my energy so. i know i owe you a lot in return for your physical labours. but this does not seem to be an exchange i can make. i wish *so* much i could do those chores myself — simple physical stuff that would be over and done, instead of these draggy unpredictable emotional miseries.

today, actually, i did make some food you might have liked. i gathered basil, parsley, yarrow, dill — chopped them up real fine and mixed in lemon juice, olive oil, tamari, tofu

< 88 >

and sunflower seeds. as i sat out on my porch eating this with chopsticks, naomi passed by. when i told her the ingredients, she said, "you should call that 'dara's elizabethan salad.' they used a lot of strong herbs like that for salads in elizabethan england."

"oh," i said, "and i suppose they also used good old elizabethan tofu?" naomi guffawed.

i like naomi a lot. i enjoy how literary she is — she's the only womon i've met in months who i can share my poems with and get really detailed criticism.

anyway, we sat there on the porch for a long time, just gabbing and sunning. the thought crossed my mind that you wouldn't like it if you passed by and saw us there. i don't want to feel that you own me, kristie.

it's been quite a while since i've come over to your place, i know. i like to see your funny trailer, with vetch and morning glories growing all over it, a living blanket of flowers. inside, i get claustrophobic. not just 'cause it's so tiny. the smell of your life, like sour milk and mildew, is heavy in there. the old photographs you've tacked on the wall — your skinny pale father in wire-rims looking severe, your sad mother. it seems gloom is your inheritance. often i've wanted to help you emerge from it, but i don't know what that would take.

people are starting to see us as individuals. i never realized the extent to which they hadn't. sanda told me that when we first came here, everyone just assumed we were lovers. not only lovers, but identical twins. because we spent so much time together and have similar values and opinions.

i laughed and said to sanda, "*we* were sure you and gwen were lovers."

"well, we sort of tried it, but it didn't work out."

"yeah — we sort of tried it too."

so now we're all nice and celibate. sometimes i feel like a nun around here, like sex is unthinkable, or that something about madrone hill discourages it. maybe it's something in the water?

when sanda left last week for california, i had a lot of

< 89 >

unexpected feelings. she hadn't even told me she was leaving so soon. i was down in the garden and she just came in the gate and said she was about to pull out. her beauty stunned me — she was wearing that thick heathery wool sweater of hers and her skin was glowing, her red hair just washed and gleaming in the sun. she had a pink rosebud peeking out of her breast pocket. but i was mad at her, too. i thought we were closer than that — i mean i would have expected her to let me know when she was planning to leave. i guess that's just how she is, though. anyway, i felt tingly just looking at her. i hope she's not gone long!

with edna off visiting her lover, that leaves just the three of us here. i think that makes naomi uncomfortable. she seems nervous because you and i came here with a definite concept of what we wanted lesbian land to be. it's not that she has a different vision. that's the thing: she and edna and sanda and gwen *didn't* have a vision, they just ended up here through various turns of fate. i wonder if they even used the word "lesbian" before we got here. they were simply "women" living on a piece of land in the country together — not a commune or collective, but as naomi says, an "unintentional community."

so here i sit on this still, hot thursday afternoon, wondering if it isn't one of those goddamn laws of the universe that no one ever loves the one who loves them. the carson mccullers syndrome, right? kristie — i don't want it to be like that. i can't love you just because you want me to. but i can question if there might be a way to stop believing — to change the rules by just stopping believing in them. i have no idea how to go about doing it. but i sense it's part of this future we're trying for, that we only get glimpses of here and there between our fears. i wish i could understand and change it all right now, soon enough to make a difference for you and me. but, my friend, i don't think that will happen. no, not this time around.

< 90 >

Caretaker Nightmares
Mickey Spencer

Colorless Rigid Empty
I am an infant I am a helpless old woman
I am difficult   My needs don't count
I can't comb my hair She is rough
      She gives up and cuts it off
      My long hair is too messy
She hurries me My shirt is on backwards
I need privacy for these struggles
She takes my art tools
      They are only sharp-edged dangers to her
      My materials only mess and junk
She cooks her way not mine
      Makes my bed the way she wants
      Puts my things where she can reach them
      Changes my life-learned details
            to suit herself
No matter how weak I become
      It is still my life
I put these nightmares on the wall
To demand power over my own life

< 91 >

Snake Woman
Allison Sletcher

batik on fabric, 34" w x 24" h

< 92 >

V

enduring

Lament to the Medical-Industrial Division of the Capitalist Patriarchal Complex

Barbara Ruth

I don't do well in hospitals
Don't interface
Appropriately
With the medical establishment.
I'm too damn queer
Have too many weird diseases.
I bristle loudly
Yell about my rights
When I'd be so much more prudent to refrain
From telling everybody
Everything about me.

I wish I at least knew
If I do it on purpose.
Is it wilfulness? Ruthlessness?
Or do I really lose
The ability to keep my mouth shut?
I mean
They cut me up
Drug me up
Shove instruments
Up and down
My openings
Then they get exasperated
When I don't play nice
When I don't bounce back
In the MediCal allotted time
For recovery.

< 95 >

I stay too long at hospitals.
Have tubes in me
At inconvenient places for the personnel
My veins
Are into non-cooperation
My brain responds idiosyncratically
To fluorescent lights
Electromagnetic fields
All that weird shit only kooks believe in.
I'm a gold mine of undocumented anecdotal side effects.
I have these codas to my surgeries
That go on and on and on
The audience gets restless
The doctors pull out their DSMs
Along with their PDRs.

Eventually, they threaten me with shrinks
It's a game we play
I say they're uninformed about my disability
They say I derive secondary benefits from my seizures
I think I exercise restraint
Not to ask about the tertiary benefits they get
From their practices.
They don't show any gratitude for my discretion
— They call me nuts
— I call them cruel
Eventually they sic the shrinks on me.

Sometimes
I hate it most of all
When the docs
Are dykes
Or gay women
Or homosexual females
Or whatever the fuck it is they will or won't admit.
It tears me up,
Because I'll knock myself out

< 96 >

Looking for the perfect, perfect words
So this time she'll really get it.
I'll invent new continents
Trying to stake out the common ground
Breathless, I'll broad jump across that chasm
Of just who it is
Who calls the shots.
Eventually I'll trust her,
Start to believe we're equals
Sister outlaws in a world we never made.
I handle it much better
When it's some straight man
Who sics the shrinks on me.

I like some docs.
The ones I like
Do what I ask them to
At least most of the time
Realize I'm both brilliant and brain-damaged
Have the good taste
To answer my questions
In my vocabulary
Like anyone would
As a common courtesy
Act like it's no big thing,
Just because they dress or talk or smile
Like regular people
Neither deny or abuse
Their power.
The docs I like
Swing pendulums
Harbour fugitives
Live in their cars
They tend to have a hard time
Keeping their privileges.

< 97 >

Sometimes I think
My ideal doc would be
A leftist crip in jail
At least as queer as I am
I'd get her out of prison
And she'd find the cure
For environmental illness.
She'd be free or freer
I'd be well or better
And then we could be companeras
Plotting to free other crips
In the sunshine.
At the ocean.
Over tea.

When I was six years old
I thought that I'd grow up
To be tortured by the state
It wasn't an erotic fantasy
Or a recurrent nightmare
— Just a fact of life
Like taking pills so I wouldn't have those fits.
Funny how long it took to realize
"The State"
Would wear white coats
Smell of alcohol and formalin
And tell me they were doing it
For my own good.

DSM — *Diagnostic and Statistical Manual* — A handbook of
        psychiatric disorders
PDR — *Physician's Desk Reference* — A handbook of
        prescription drugs

< 98 >

she worked
Pauline Rankin

where there were thousands of people, every minute hour
new faces, voices, talking, yelling, demanding and she had to
stare at a green screen machine, push in programmed digits no
place go hide scream aw fuck no air just conditioning just
numbers and faces and people she didn't know leaving to fly in
airplanes to places just flashing back at her looming vdt no
place to go no cool grass below bare feet no children's voices,
crayola colours singing and and and ... she was in hell but it
was her job her job her job and   and   and

she tells the doctor
I hate my job
it makes me sick

he gives her pills
to cure her 40 hour a week disease

< 99 >

Asthmatic Conditions
Ayasha Mayr Handel

Somehow my body has come to curse me
unable to breathe
sometimes unable to leave my bed in the morning
punishment encroaches itself upon me.

The arms on the clock spin
as days pass into my memory
for every day passed,
I am faced with a burden of proof.
I am refused any acknowledgement
until I can justify these days
filled with "inaction,"
filled with a passive nothingness
unrecognizable in form.

My productivity is gauged by them
and I am silently suffocating on their terms.

Medical records do not mention all the ways
my lungs have affected me
the way they've torn up my psychology
and *cursed* me.

Struggle remains unrecognized
unnoticed
unseen.
Hidden in my closet with the bloody rags I had to cough into
the pill bottles littering the floor
food I couldn't eat
clothes that wouldn't fit me anymore.
Days filtered through my vomiting.

< 100 >

These precious details remain
unspoken
unrecorded
like a silent picture
turning itself over and over in the reels of my memory

Treated as though I'm a bloody liar
— *she can't be trusted* —
They treat what is unseen as unreal
or simply my surreal creation —
the twisted figment of my imagination
while I pass day over day subsumed by the fear of those images
and their return.
Suddenly aware of dust, moldy spores
and all the particles which tear at *every* part of me.

As my voice roughens and fades I realize that "breaking
the silence" is not an equal access ideal
When I cannot or choose not to speak my experience is
subverted
bound by the demarcation of un-spoken realities.
It is not with the privilege of choice I remain silent
how can I scream when I cannot
Breathe!

she screamed at me poking me measuring what she could
of me Dr. Smart told me
I had anxiety they think I'm a hypochondriac they want
me to take off *all* my clothes
memories of fingers on my breasts my breasts pressed up
against the glass for my x-ray
fingers shoved up my cunt with no gloves hands all over
my bare back and chest
he refuses to treat me until I take off my shirt and I
almost start to cry again
and now I am crying they all wonder why I haven't been
to see the specialists...more hands
grabbing for a piece of me and I'm the one who's
Sick (?).

< 101 >

The wheezing and rasping kept her awake at night
(window into my fear)
so I get another inhaler
steroids so my lungs won't bleed
bronchodilators
Pulmicort and Salbutamol for health.

She is afraid I will die.
I am only afraid this will go on forever.
She holds me hoping to squeeze some breath into me
(Salbutamol)
my body shakes with a slight hysteria
in this way my anger speaks — in the mid of the night
when I am beyond sleep.

I cannot go back from where I came
I cannot go on as though I am unchanged
as though illness were isolated
as though I was not consumed by it
as though I will never be again
as though I've forgotten
all their hands on me and in me
tubes going where only my dis-ease had ever gone
where my condition lives inside of me
where the smoke goes,
like some kind of faulty "feminized" suicide attempt
(which rarely works)
like a bottle of pills without alcohol.
Sometimes when people ask I simply say;
"it's stress-related."

Asthma — like something common
Allergies — like something bothersome and vague
the words pass smoothly over the tongue
no hint of how they've torn my lungs apart
how my lungs have torn my life apart

< 102 >

how the days have slipped by unrecognized
how I've been depressed
how at times I become immobilized
pained with nausea
no one could touch me
breathe my poisoned air
I couldn't move or touch the bed sheets
without throwing up
everything.
  How thin my frame became.
  How diminished I felt.
How weak I felt after rising out of bed after ten days of
living there
I almost fell down the stairs.

(perhaps I lost the weight because I was too weak to carry it)

Now that I can walk again,
they expect that all is forgotten.

— *Parlez rien.*
— *Entendez rien.*
— *Rappelez-vous rien.*

Comme c'est possible.
As though I am unmarked.

     I have developed phobias of viruses, basements, my
     uncommon cold, strep throat, the measles, pneumonia,
            viral tracheitis, bronchitis and the flu.

They bury themselves deep into my flesh
will not let me go for weeks at a time
eat at my flesh
eat at me
until I feel like there is nothing of *me* left
As though my body is only a skeleton
my identity has been drawn out with the blood in viles.

< 103 >

My substance
in *their* lab
separated into its composites
tested
and then discarded.

I don't even get to touch.

It is not with the privilege of choice I remain silent.
How can I scream when I cannot *breathe*?

Now that I can walk again,
they expect that all is forgotten.
As though I am unmarked.

< 104 >

Anger
Allison Sletcher

batik on fabric, 28" w x 20" h

< 105 >

Sleight of Hand
Andrea Broc Lowe

for Isabel

Do they really think
we will always lie down for them

under their blade
or tip our heads back
open our mouths wide
to swallow their pills
like swallowing knives

or lying down
on a bed of nails.

We're not meant to die
from this
but you did
just by swallowing
their promises.

I can hear them now
    such a shame, a pity
    the poor woman
    a classic example
    a primary case
    a typical fusion of pain and madness

Surely they tried
to help her
they did so much
everything they could

every trick
in the book.

< 106 >

Stop Feeling or You'll Never Be Normal Again: My Life With Cancer Since Lump Day

Kathleen Martindale

Part 1: 18 February 1992; revised again and again, never to be finished until I die.

Does the world really need another cancer narrative? No, not really, not if what I'm writing is merely vanity ethnography. But, in a cultural climate where even implicitly feminist discourses about breast cancer, such as *Dr. Susan Love's Breast Book* (1991), are still ignored by both the medical cancer establishment and the very popular new age self-help counter-establishment which smugly blames victims and gets away with it, lesbian testimonials to the experiences of multiple stigmatization that those of us with breast cancer face are rarely heard.

And so I see myself as writing in what is beginning to seem like a tradition, that of the lesbian crying in the wilderness, attempting to reach other lesbians, primarily, in order to warn them about this epidemic. Act up or it might be your turn next. As Sandra Butler puts it in the introduction to *Cancer in Two Voices* (1991), quoting Barbara Rosenblum, her lover, who was misdiagnosed and ultimately died of metastatic cancer caused by medical malpractice, "Many of my friends will see their future in the way I handle mine. There will be others. It's only a matter of time."

It's no accident that the two best, most moving, and most politically astute analyses of the havoc that the American cancer establishment has created were written by lesbian feminists: Audre Lorde's *The Cancer Journals* (1980) and Sandra Butler and Barbara Rosenblum's *Cancer in Two Voices* (1991). Apparently, these works are unknown to the cancer establishment literature. Although Susan Love (the implicitly feminist breast surgeon and cancer action advocate) includes Lorde in her book, even she does not mention the far more disturbing book by Butler and Rosenblum. Non- or anti-feminist

< 107 >

cancer literature is upbeat and apolitical; by contrast, (heterosexual) feminist narratives are full of tragi-comic anecdotes about medical chicanery. In between stories about the foibles of their husbands and boyfriends (the major players in their lives), these writers sardonically attack the insensitivities and stupidities of the cancer establishment and suggest what is wrong with the way that cancer is treated in North America. Quietly heroic in their fight against the disease, as well as the doctors who mistreat it and them, those writers do not tend to think in terms of mounting a collective analysis or struggle against both. Lesbian feminist narratives do and for that reason they are both more painful, and more political. They are therefore also more likely to be marginalized in both of those official discourses on breast cancer. Thus, I write, adding my small voice to what I hope will become a din which can't be ignored.

I never tell a story straight, especially not the first time. Telling it "straight" is an act of consideration; but these days I'm inconsiderate. More accurately, I'm furious. I'm getting ahead of myself even so.

New Year's Eve 1991. The transition time. 1991: a truly horrific year for the world, but for me personally, it was a time of great happiness and fulfilment. I was beginning to get used to the difference between my sense of what was going on outside of me (which for me means the macro-political world) and what was going on in my personal, that is, psychological and individual life. What was going on outside of me, and what was going on in my personal life, used to be much more confused. Not that it really mattered, they were both terrible.

Melody, my lover, who's made my life flourish, and I spent New Year's Eve together with a friend. Usually, I spend some part of this evening alone and review the past year and meditate on the state of the world and my small part in it. I think that I must have felt some dread on this particular New Year's Eve but I'm not sure whether I'm reading back more drama than was actually there.

New Year's Day plus one was devoted to grading student

< 108 >

papers. I save the worst stuff for the last part of the holidays. If I've got a month "off," I want a lot of variety and something to show for it. First, I spent a week at a yoga ashram where I replenished myself after the fall term of paper-writing and teaching, that is, trying to disturb complacent young women about gender and other injustices and offering comfort to the other ones who inspire me. Then I went to Montréal for a week to write a paper on lesbian ethics with a friend. I came home with forty-four (same as my age) manuscript pages and a hell of an editing job to do.

My friend works part-time at a really awful university. She is desperate for a permanent job but is unwilling to work as hard as I. She thinks that I take work too seriously and should lighten up. I think she thinks that when I found love, I should have become less intense. Maybe she thinks that's why I got cancer. Certainly is a popular idea. Maybe it is why I got cancer.

Stress. Like most people who are "different" and who have few, if any, material resources, I really had had my share of it. First, I had chosen to incarnate this time in an extremely dysfunctional politically repressive working-class Irish-Catholic family. Second, I underwent plenty of stress when I lived in a Montréal slum where I was harassed by male tenants and the concierge, as well as when I fought for my job and lost out to a wife and mom who did more "mainstream" work than I did. I later experienced more of the same when I found out that my ex-chair had written a lesbian-baiting letter of reference when I had applied for the job that I did get in 1988. The gratuitously nasty letter, which might have been actionable, was written two years after I had been forced to leave his department, and the congenial exciting city of Montréal, in order to take a job directing women's studies in Calgary.

Some of the Montréal stress was material, and came from trying to live on $10,000 a year less on my first "real, full-time" job than I did when I had three "part-time" teaching and organizing jobs in Toronto; from being forced to take out a loan to pay additional taxes amounting to

< 109 >

$17,000 on a $28,000 salary (for a job which I almost didn't get because my previous employer of seven years had "no record" of me); from flying, driving, bussing (or some combination thereof) every two weeks to spend time with my then-girlfriend; from eating fried eggs for dinner (I was too tired to cook proper vegetarian food), and drinking a couple of beers to calm down enough to sleep after I came home from teaching at eleven at night (which I did all year because my contract was for ten months and I never knew whether, or what, I would teach from one term to the next). With all that stress, I could have planted the seeds of the undifferentiated carcinoma that I first discovered on Lump Day, January 2, 1992.

Like nearly all of the other women who've written breast cancer narratives, I can point to flaws in my character, risks I've taken with my health, and bad judgements I've made, generally, that might have made me a candidate for the disease. Listening to the siren call of the now-popular new age psychobabble approach to "you brought it on yourself" diseases such as cancer and AIDS, the approach taken by the Simontons, Marianne Williamson, Louise Le Hay and Bernie Siegel, I too have pondered whether I just might have the cancer personality: I'm too nice, too good a girl.

Sometimes I get confused, though. I am, and have been, a woman who loves too much. I also work too much and therefore have a Type A personality. I just _____ (verb) too much. Now, the possibility that I might be too good is hard for me to believe. I've been accused of many things, but too good? Never. Not even just plain good, or good enough. Whatever it is, though, it must have something to do with doing it or being it too much. Maybe I'm a working-class (essentialist) over-achieving, intellectual dyke who _____ too much. Excess must be the key to it all. Thank god, at last I've come up with a medical etiology that's got interesting literary implications. Maybe I can become "mainstream" in English departments yet. Maybe acting out of material necessity (real or perceived) causes cancer. According to that "logic," none of my bourgeois colleagues will get cancer.

< 110 >

That's simply not true. Maybe the class-resentment that I feel caused the cancer. Maybe the fact that I'm not-nice caused it.

Anyhow, it was January 2 and I was grading papers. They were much better than I had expected them to be. I had about seventy to do, and I intended to do them in three long days, then take the weekend off. School resumed on Tuesday. I had everything under control.

All of Wednesday, my right breast ached. The pain felt as if it were right near the surface. I ignored it. I was mid-cycle, so it didn't seem to be connected with my period; anyway, slightly painful breasts pre-menstruation had become a thing of the past since I had stopped drinking coffee in August. Oh, the pure life which I led. Under control, that's me. When I finished twenty or so papers, I went for a ride on the exercise bike to relax. The pain increased. Melody came home from work and I told her it hurt. Why not look at it? I pulled up my sweaty t-shirt and there it was: a visible small protrusion with some redness on the upper outside part of my right breast. With evidence visible, I allowed myself to feel pain. Took two aspirins then, two more four hours later. No change in the pain. I'd call the doctor tomorrow.

I did not feel any particular confidence in the medical help we have sought at the clinic in the past year. While the doctors have not been stupid or sexist, they've been uninterested in my complaints about having unusually frequent and difficult-to-shake colds. After I had had four bad ones with laryngitis, I wondered whether my immune system might have been compromised. The doctor scoffed off this suggestion. According to him, four colds a year are nothing, to be expected (although never before known in my experience).

In most of the cancer narratives (such as, Gilda Radner's *It's Always Something*), the narrator feels as if something is the matter with her long before the doctors find anything that would confirm this belief. She goes from doctor to doctor, from test to test. It's nothing, nothing, nothing, all in your head, they say, until they find the cancer; and by then, of course, it's too late for you. You're terminal. You've acted

< 111 >

responsibly, been assertive, had the material advantages to fight the medical system, and you still wind up a cancer statistic. And the band plays on.

On that day, January 3, a doctor whom I had never seen before examined my lump. He called in yet another doctor. They agreed; there was a lump. They made an appointment for me for the following Monday (very fast in economic disaster-zone Ontario) at the Breast Centre, Women's College Hospital. When they told me this, I noticed that to get their info — "it's a lump" — they had consulted a Ciba pamphlet on breast cancer. I knew those pamphlets by heart from my running days of running injuries. (I've run eight marathons; in my case, low body fat and intense regular exercising did not ward off breast cancer.) They're very basic, and I wasn't impressed with my doctors' knowledge base.

The weekend was an anxious time and not at all what I had anticipated my time off to be like. We didn't know then that nothing would be the same ever again. We didn't tell anyone yet.

Monday I went to the Breast Centre. In the crowded waiting room, where the anxiety is profound and entirely ignored, no woman talks to any other. After a couple of hours' wait, I'm called into the surgeon's office. She makes small talk. I start to play patient, not realizing that I'm changing epistemological and actuarial categories forever. She tries to aspirate the lump. Instead of what I've read is supposed to come out (a lot of greenish yucch), she's only able to extract a little bloody lymphatic stuff. (I had bought *Dr. Susan Love's Breast Book* the day before, but only read the good parts, the parts before she gets to the diagrams of mastectomies, because I really am an optimist after all, which I've just been finding out since I met Melody two and a half years ago.) Not good, she says, and I know enough to agree.

I put my shirt back on and she starts to tell me that "we" have three possibilities for treatment: total mastectomy, total with radiation, and partial with radiation. I ask her a question of clarification. Why is she telling me this? Is she sharing her philosophy of treatment with me because she has an urge to

< 112 >

talk or because she has reason to believe that I will need to do something with this information imminently? (I'm not sure whether I use the word "imminently.") She says "yes" to the latter; she believes that I have a carcinoma. There, the word's out. Okay. I'm cool as she draws the diagrams. I collect information for a living so I (almost) never pass up the chance to look at diagrams. Same as it ever was.

She tells me that she'll send me for blood work, another mammogram, an ultrasound, and a chest X-ray. I'll come back next week for a biopsy. Ever the optimist, I think that the biopsy can be done under local anaesthetic in her office. No, I'll have to be admitted to the hospital. General anaesthesia. If it's benign, I'll go home that night. If it isn't, she'll remove the tumour, do an axial dissection of the lymph nodes under my arm and then "we" will wait for the test results to see if it's metastasized. On my way out, I ask her for a prescription for valium. I will need it. Yoga and medication and a loving, intelligent partner are all on my side but I still think I'll need the valium. And I did; in fact, for the next ten months, I won't sleep without medication.

On the way to the other building for the tests, I have the first opportunity to be alone. I believe that I'm fine, I'm under control, I'm with other people. I tell myself that I'll feel things when it's safe to do so. Not now, not here. Hospitals are not safe places. I call Melody at work and give her the news, requesting that she come to get me as soon as possible. It's hard to sound under control as I, for the first time, articulate the situation to another human being. The only other human being?

The mammogram is particularly painful and the technician typically, but unintentionally, brutal. Must be a terrible job. Foucault would love to see his work so confirmed as it is when I numb myself entirely to assume the role of the body under medical scrutiny. Melody arrives. She drives us home. Usually I drive. First loss of control. There'll be others, I have no idea, still, now, I have no idea how many of them there will be, nor what they'll entail.

Welcome to the Cancer Club. Sometimes it seems like just

< 113 >

another women's group. Although breast cancer will affect one in eight North American women, the doctors are still using the same ineffective treatments that they used forty years ago. Now I'm about to go down the garden path with them. I'm writing this so that other lesbians will know more than I did, and so that maybe you'll have the strength to fight back before it happens to you too.

The time between Monday, January 6 (when I first see the surgeon) and Tuesday, January 24 (when I'm admitted to the hospital) goes very fast. After the surgery and diagnosis, I tell just a few people. I'm afraid that the English department will not give me tenure because of the diagnosis. That is, they will use the diagnosis in order to get rid of me but the real reasons will be that I do radical stuff, and I'm a lesbian. It would be a perfect excuse for them. I don't tell some acquaintances, even friends, if they've got their own miseries. I tell the ones whom I trust the most and whom I believe care about me. But most don't want to know. I've lost friends because of this. As a friend with metastasized breast cancer says, when people find out you have cancer, they don't see you as yourself in this particular situation; they see you in terms of their own projections and memories about every cancer "victim" they've ever known. In other words, they imagine you either as someone soon to be dead, or as a brave Terry Fox clone. Really, though, they don't want to imagine you at all. Each time you tell people what you've got, your phone rings less frequently, and your friends get busy. (But I don't know this yet. Now you do.)

When I come to consciousness in the recovery room, I check the clock. It says 6:35 p.m. I lost consciousness at 3:15 p.m. Too long for it to be benign. The man in the bed next to me is screaming. They are mispronouncing his name: "Bog-dan. Bog-dan." When I discover the little sac which is attached to my body and is collecting fluid, I know for sure. It's called a hemovac and it collects drainage from the lymph node removal. They wouldn't have done that if the lump had been benign. Logical inference: my always dependable ally.

First word to Melody: "Facts!" (What a strange choice of

< 114 >

language! I know there are no facts; but then, of course, I'm not a real literary person.) Tone: imperious.

My memory, factual and emotional, or whatever you call it, is not too clear about my next three days in the hospital. I remember, and Melody tells me, that I seemed in some ways normal for me: impatient, using my hands to indicate that she should "go faster" with her information about the diagnosis. When she had told me all that she knew, I think that I became quiet, or maybe I began to be verbally morbid and angry. I keep forgetting. This cannot be a factual account; maybe I am trying to be literary. Maybe I can get a publication out of it.

The next day I was angry.

The day after I was despondent.

In general, I'd have a hard time saying which emotion I am better at feeling. If I think about all of the people that I've known well, I'd have to say that I'm at the top, or very near the top when it comes to anger and despair. What might confuse you about the way in which I feel these things is that I keep on working them through. I mean, I keep on doing stuff. I don't take to my bed or scream at anyone even when those things seem like the logical ones to do. And, even while I'm feeling extremely angry and despondent, I have no difficulty feeling great joy about sunshine, dogs jumping in the air, or people being kind to each other even if no one notices. As I've said, the way that I feel these things confuses most people. I really don't know why it does, but it does.

When I first came home from the hospital, I seemed okay in a superficial way. I recovered fast from the surgery and was back in the classroom the very next week. The breast wound was healing fast; the underarm more slowly. It was painful to write on the blackboard. Waiting for the test-results was trying. Tuesday night, January 21, the surgeon left a message on our answering machine for me to call her the next morning. Nothing else. We spent a horrible night contemplating my imminent death. We thought the fact that

< 115 >

she had said nothing was ominous; but we were wrong. Just typical doctor insensitivity.

The tumour had been the size of a walnut. (Jokes about walnuts have become very popular at our house.) I'm 100% "walnut free" (or so we hope). The surgeon called the next morning, just as I had to ready myself to go to school and to play normal. She said the margins were close (they remove the tumour as far as possible, and as far as they can see it, then send it to pathology to be sure), but they were clean, and all the tests were negative. No metastases. Melody and I cried for joy quite a bit. I hope I always remember that moment because how much we love each other was never so clear and so precious. Ten minutes before the surgeon had called, I couldn't imagine how I could go teach and play normal with death so seemingly imminent.

After the first surgery, as I got used to living in a crisis, I slowly began to feel again. Getting cancer has changed me in many ways. Like all of the women who've written cancer narratives, I've changed my diet: now it's very low calorie and low fat macrobiotic vegetarian. Although I've been a vegetarian for a quarter of a century, apparently it wasn't enough to avoid cancer. Making these dietary changes has not really been an intellectual decision, but following what my body craves.

You'd think that since I've been a vegetarian for so long, I'd have gotten used to being socially different with regard to the very culturally important acts of buying, preparing, and consuming food. But no, as if it were a state that I'm just entering, I feel that I'm a freak. Not eating meat, not smoking, not drinking caffeine and almost no alcohol was bad enough. (I hate purer than thou fascists of the body even though I could easily be confused with them. I do what I do or don't do for ethical reasons, ones which I try as much as possible to keep to myself because talking about such stuff is silly and futile.) Now, there's almost nothing which I can eat in a restaurant, and I see skulls and crossbones on everyday and previously beloved items such as, olive oil, olives, avocadoes, and butter.

< 116 >

Since the two of us are known to "take good care of" our health, it is possible that my situation might be perceived by other people, as well as by myself as a sign of god's punishment, or as the cancer-personality syndrome. Cancer presents enormous opportunities for people like me who have a talent for obsessing. Sometimes, when I get a momentary sense of what the yoga people call "witness consciousness," I can see all at once the incredible mind-games and guilt-tripping that I'm laying on myself, but it too passes.

I'm now more angry, more despairing, and more spontaneous, sometimes to the point of utterly surprising myself. Cancer has made me even more of a lesbian, that is, an outlaw from polite heterosexist society. In fact, this document is evidence of it. I write and re-write this narrative for hours non-stop. Everything too much.

It's February 18 when I write this the first time. February 18: Black lesbian feminist poet warrior and cancer survivor Audre Lorde's birthday and, coincidentally, this document has just happened. [In December 1992, when I edit and update it yet again, Audre's dead and I'm recovering from a double mastectomy that I apparently didn't need, so there's lots more to tell.] If only I had the literary art to let you know the difference in feeling, in dread, and in suffering, from sentence to sentence, from hour to hour, from one murderous cancer treatment to another...

It's reading week. I wanted to go away but my plans were ruined because I had to see two oncologists and radiation specialists. Yesterday I saw the radiation specialist at the Princess Margaret Hospital. Melody came too. The appointment was for 8:40 a.m. You can tell that I'm still a beginner at this because I still get angry when it's like the military: hurry up and wait. A standardized consent form for the radiation was among the forms that I was initially handed. When I said that I wanted to talk to the doctor about the radiation, a little *red* slip was attached to the unsigned form. First flag of a non-cooperator, as I was about to find out.

Until the doctor came in at 11:00 a.m., the nurses did just about nothing. We had been sitting in an examining room

< 117 >

for forty-five minutes. They had asked me to fill out a questionnaire, the object of which was unclear to me, but which I had filled out dutifully; it included questions about which mode of transportation you will use to get to the appointments, and how you feel in response to the diagnosis. As the doctor examined me, her nurse read through my answers. I had told the nurse I felt ambivalent about getting radiated because of what I had read about it, and that I had already talked to another doc who opposes it utterly.

I don't remember exactly when, or how, the shit began to hit the fan between me and the tiny, young doctor. I think it began with my questions about side-effects. I am (consciously) most concerned about experiencing extreme fatigue, didn't want to miss any teaching, and I certainly didn't want to change my after-the-term-ends plans of a research-packed, writing-intensive summer. [From the vantage point of December 1992: Ha! You fool. You still think your life runs on your "normal" time-table.] In December 1991, I had sent a book proposal to Routledge, and the tenure process was going to start during the next year. Diseased lesbian marxists need not apply.

As the doctor began to give me the basics about radiation (which I already knew), she said that it differed from low-dosage radiation, which she admitted is dangerous. Apparently, high-dosage radiation which is very carefully aimed in 21 sessions [a bargain; according to my reading of Dr. Susan Love's book, I was up for 25 zaps, plus a mega-dose or "boost"], some aimed at a "small" part of your lung, is not dangerous at all. Since I'm a trained literary critic, I usually can recognize irony or humour; but she didn't seem to be having fun. Neither was I.

I objected, saying that it was emotionally difficult for me to voluntarily present myself for treatments that seemed potentially dangerous (I knew all of the experts admit that no dosage of radiation is "safe"), and that are described like torture in the literature that I had read, and I continued to press for information about side-effects. She insisted that there would be none except for some fatigue which she

< 118 >

assured me would disappear within two weeks of the treatments' conclusion. I indicated that I was not pleased with the fact that treatments for breast cancer were primitive, that survival rates had not increased in the last forty years, that the incidence in North America had increased recently to one in three women, and that this situation would not be tolerated if breast cancer happened to men. She told me that I had read too much. (It's the "too" syndrome again.) She objected to the way in which I had described the treatments as primitive and said that I had insulted the medical profession. I asked her how she could sleep at night given the state of cancer research and cancer results. She said everything is fine. She objected to my observation that not enough money is spent on breast cancer research and said that spending more money is not the solution: the human body is complicated.

She advised me to be co-operative and not to display my "militancy" in the hospital, where it would get me into trouble. She implied that bad things happen to people who don't cooperate. Not with her, mind you, but with some of the other medical people; she was giving me this piece of information out of kindness. Once again, I felt that warm and special bond that comes from experiencing the universal sisterhood of women and I recognized the difference that female admission to the professions makes.

We left. I went to the gym and worked out as hard as I could. I was so angry that I didn't experience fatigue. I could not beat up the Stairmaster, the Nautilus machine, nor the exercise bicycle. When I came home, I phoned the Cancer Society and asked for information about Breast Cancer Action, a "militant" new group that a friend had told me about. (I wanted to be able to tell Dr. Fei Fei, the radiation true-believer, that I had immediately joined the group because of her.) The Cancer Society didn't have any information then but I'll keep trying because that's what non-cooperators do.

So, dear lesbian reader, I hope that you don't mind my anger and despair: I'm waiting for radiation to begin but I

< 119 >

don't know exactly when that will be. It's difficult to plan your life when no one who has power over you will tell you anything. But that's how it goes when you've got cancer. I have exactly as much information about it now as I did when I went into Princess Margaret Hospital, that is, what I've managed to get from talking to friends and reading (too many) books. It's probably the sensible thing to do, that is, to submit to being zapped; but I'm not scientifically competent enough to weigh the odds. On Thursday, I will see another oncologist. This one's female too. She will decide whether I need adjuvant therapy, that is, chemotherapy. Chemotherapy, now that's real torture!

I hope this doc will be different from the other doctors I've seen so far. With very few exceptions, physicians are the most conformist and complacent people I've ever met. I sometimes wonder how they get that way. Born or made? Made at what points? Although I've read (too many) books about the making of a this or that kind of doc, I still don't understand. That it's a useful defense in their line of work, I can believe. Actually, I have a lot of respect for denial, and I strive to remember, when I'm criticizing others for using it, how good I am at it. So far, the cancer experience has brought to the fore my most primitive and habitual defense mechanisms.

Maybe this doc will be a little bit psychologically sensitive; maybe she will know how to talk to me. By now, I'm not expecting much. At least maybe she'll give me a timetable, or maybe she'll be able to explain (in a way that makes sense to me) why she wants to do things to my body. I don't expect her to be caring or compassionate; just to be able to justify her actions. They call it "the scientific method." It's why they get paid so much compared to literary critics. Similes are easy; I want facts. I can do the interpretations myself. Keeps me busy and into trouble.

It feels as if it's time to stop now. Clearly, as with everything else that I say or do, I could go on and on with my thoughts about my own mortality; but I don't think I have anything interesting to say about it yet. I'm still too spiritually

< 120 >

shallow. After all, anger and despair are my strong suits. And, remember, my prognosis is very good — seventy-five percent or even more of something or other. Maybe five years' survival. Enough to write a book, get tenure and let Melody and a few other people know how much I love them.

Part 2: 27 December 1992; today I lost another friendship over cancer.

I've changed my mind. Because of what happened to me next, I feel that I have to write even more, and in an even angrier tone. If I ended my story on the upbeat, as Amy Gross and Dee Ito, the editors of *Women Talk About Breast Surgery: From Diagnosis to Recovery* do, I'd be misleading you. The book is relentlessly positive, but I see from glancing at it that Gross and Ito already edited *Women Talk About Gynecological Surgery*, so they've got a good thing going: as long as women have "female troubles," they're in business.

Gross and Ito interviewed a bunch of middle class women (almost all of whom were white and straight) who are breast cancer survivors. These privileged women are the editors' models of the "new patient" who fights the establishment — and wins! They use these true stories of "women's" breast cancer experience in order to claim that it is a very manageable one if you, the patient, take charge. This is a deadly fantasy, not the least of all because it disguises the editors' racist, classist, sexist, and homophobic agenda. I don't want to lend support to it in any way.

Like me, their interviewees read as much as they could about breast cancer and became experts on their disease. Like the good girls that they are, they insist that errors which they have made — bad diets and too much stress — caused their illness, rather than environmental pollution or just some unknown combination of genes, pollution, lifestyle, and bad luck. Unlike me, everything goes well for these women. Not so coincidentally, none of them has metastatic cancer or a "bad" prognosis. Socialist feminist Barbara Ehrenreich endorsed this book. Why'd she do it?

After mastectomies, all these happy heterosexuals had

< 121 >

reconstructive plastic surgery to give them back the boobs that society and their hubbies craved. Breast reconstruction is expensive and generally involves a lengthy series of painful operations in which expanders are put under the skin of the chest wall, and then foreign substances (some of them known to be carcinogenic) are implanted. The implants make it more difficult to detect recurrences too. Skin is grafted from other parts of the body to make new mounds. Sometimes, through the use of dyes or tattooing, simulated nipples are created. Unsafe, probably; ridiculous, maybe; heterosexist, surely.

Although by now I'm pretty used to reading medical atrocity stories, descriptions of breast reconstruction are not for the faint of stomach. All of these obvious objections to them are, however, finessed by Gross and Ito. According to them and their interviewees, deciding to have a reconstruction is a sign of having a positive body-image post-mastectomy. Run that logic by me again! Of course, the surgeons stress that the mastectomies (that's what they call us) should have a "realistic" attitude about what these fake boobs will look like. That is, ghastly. "Half a grapefruit," with scars. A feminist analysis of all of this never occurs to the women interviewed, nor to their medical establishment-friendly editors.

Gross and Ito's manufactured happy endings are nothing like the tragic story of the medical negligence which killed lesbian academic Barbara Rosenblum, as lovingly, if harrowingly recounted, in diary form by her lover, Sandra Butler in *Cancer in Two Voices*. It's the hardest book that I've ever read. Read it only when you're up to it, but do read it. It's more than a cancer narrative; it's a lesbian love story. Nor could Gross and Ito (or any of the medical establishment they pimp for) allow in their book a hint of the political analysis of the ugly combination of breast fetishism/mammary directed heterosexism that Audre Lorde produced in *The Cancer Journals*.

What happened to me after my first surgery in January 1992 is that I submitted my body to twenty-eight zaps of radiation. Radiation might or might not help prevent recur-

< 122 >

rences of cancer, but it is certainly quite effective at turning you into a cancer patient. Going to the hospital, at their convenience, every week for five weeks makes it very hard to lead a normal work-life, and the way in which you are treated (like a piece of meat) very effectively destroys your emotional well-being and induces fear, and impotent rage.

If you're a lesbian, there's no psychological or social support. All of the cancer pamphlets in hospital waiting rooms are written for heterosexual, indeed, married women. The biggest problem for women with mastectomies, according to Cancer Society lore, is the possibility, no, the likelihood, that their husbands will leave them, or will become sexually dysfunctional because "their" woman is "deformed."

The heterosexists who run support groups fail to notice that the needs of lesbians are different from that of the married middle-class housewives for whom they design their therapy. Our social worker got back to us on the lesbian question (whether there were any others in the groups, whether the leaders had ever had lesbians in the groups, whether we would be treated like a couple) *ten* weeks after we had called seeking help. They complacently assured us that although they had never before knowingly had a lesbian with cancer in their groups, we wouldn't be rejected because this was a big city and the patients were fairly young and therefore would be "tolerant." We declined, horrified.

The oncologist, another woman, was far more responsive than the surgeon or radiation doc. She recommended six months of chemotherapy (something that they now routinely advise for women with early breast cancer), then she left on maternity leave. My case was passed on to a male oncologist, who turned out to be the only compassionate doctor I encountered during my ordeal. He seemed willing to talk and to listen.

Chemo was not the nightmare that I expected it to be. It was another, and far subtler, one. Each time I went to the hospital for the i.v. treatments which pumped poisons through my veins, brought on early menopause, and destroyed my immune system, I felt as if I were not only

< 123 >

desecrating my body, but that I was also giving it over to my enemies: the medical establishment. Why, then, did I do it? I felt that I had no alternative. I already do all the alternative lifestyle stuff — I meditate, exercise, do yoga, eat healthy food, think positive thoughts and, yet, I got cancer.

I was heavily invested in doing chemo "well." I read the Bernie Siegel books and tried to imagine the chemo drugs as healing energies, if not precisely the "white knights" that he recommends (they made me think of the Ku Klux Klan); but this is as easy to believe as it is to believe that cops are my friends, and that "family values" are good for women and children. The chemo drugs might have been killing cancer cells, but that didn't make them my buddies. I saw the months of chemo as some kind of ultramarathon. The key was to endure it, and not ask why you're doing it in the first place.

Doing chemo well meant not heaving my guts out, and in that limited sense, I guess I did do well. I never vomited, but I had what I called "background nausea" two weeks out of four, and lived in a strange grey state of terror and weakness for the duration. Some of my hair fell out, and what remained had the brittle and fragile texture of corn silk. We called it "Chemo hair." I lost my appetite, a lot of weight, and got my hair cut short, anticipating baldness. Chemotherapy is best described as a period of prolonged, and yet anticipatory, mourning.

In addition to the IV drugs, I took three nitrogen mustard-like pills (you might have heard about this stuff in connection with World War I chemical warfare) every two weeks out of four. I'd meditate before taking them in order to psych myself up for the self-poisoning. I never lost the feeling of profound conflict about what I was doing to myself. Of course, you don't know whether chemotherapy has worked until you have a recurrence, then, as with all of the other cancer treatments, you know it hasn't.

In mid-July, half-way through chemo, the jolly girl guide radiation doc examined me and thought I had grown more cancerous lumps. She consulted with the surgeon and I was

< 124 >

called in quite suddenly. The surgeon stupidly did a needle biopsy first, the resulting contamination of which made it impossible to do a mammogram for another ten days. Even before all of the results were back, and with no hesitation, or sensitivity, she told me that she had bad news: the biopsy indicated the presence of cancer cells. She examined me to see how much she'd have to cut. She estimated thirty per cent of my right breast was filled with lumps. Doing another lumpectomy wasn't wise. This time, it would have to be a mastectomy. Because she was going away on holidays, I would have to wait with the time-bomb ticking inside me for three weeks. She dismissed me.

If life had seemed rough in the months from January to mid-July, nothing prepared me for life after recurrence fever. I had been seeing a female therapist who specialized in cancer. She charged $120 for 50 minutes, which I could only afford because I'm lucky enough to have extensive medical coverage. She abandoned me to go on her holidays and left no back-up. I tried to get a second opinion. Having cancer is bad enough at any time, but it's definitely inconvenient in the summer. Very few surgeons were available, and, since this is an epidemic, those who were available, were very busy. When the lump became painful, I pleaded with the oncologist that he have another surgeon examine me. The new one did, very cursorily. Without any of my recent records in front of him, he testily informed me that everything was fine. The tumour would not metastasize during the delay. There was nothing to worry about. He dismissed me.

Did I mourn for my breasts? No, not exactly. I was afraid they were killing me. I wanted them gone. A gay male colleague suggested that this wouldn't be as hard for me as it would be for a het woman. People (who can't get cancer) say the funniest things. "Them," that's right. I decided to have both of them off because I feared that I would ultimately need to have more surgery anyhow, and because I wanted my body, or what remained of it, to be symmetrical.

On September 2, 1992, I had a bilateral mastectomy. The hospital stay was more like a farce, except that it went on

< 125 >

in intensive care, because my heart had developed an irregular heartbeat. From being compromised by the effects of the chemo? Who knows? From this point in my narrative, if not from the very beginning, everything I say about what happened to me, and why it happened, is conjecture.

I have tried to learn the logic under which my surgeon acted, but she has skilfully evaded answering my questions directly. Although she did express a bit of chagrin when she admitted that the surgery had been unnecessary, she followed it up by drawing a diagram that she uses to teach medical students about mortality statistics. Smugly, she informed me that in the long run we all die. What that has to do with what she did to me is unclear to me.

So, it seems that I did not need the mastectomies, and that I had not had a recurrence. In the recovery room I thought that this was what the surgeon was trying to tell me, but I wasn't sure because I was still woozy from the anaesthetic. When I told Melody about what the doc had said, or rather, implied, we called her into the hospital room. She said that during the surgery she could see no visible signs of cancer but had cut my breasts off anyway. Just following orders. My words, obviously, my beliefs that you should take responsibility for your actions, and my concepts of what should constitute medical competence. But doesn't. Do I have grounds for suing? Probably not. (Wilful not knowing is the name of the game with breast cancer.) Probably, my life not being hers, she is content to say "*we* [not I] don't know" and "*we* [not I] did the best *we* [not I] could."

I remembered what I had said to the other doctor: how do they sleep at night? The immediate results from pathology showed no signs of cancer either. When all the results came back, ten days later, there was still no sign of the cancer. Good luck, eh? I didn't have cancer. Now I've got an invisible disability. Can't go to the gym anymore. Probably can't play squash. Most people would cringe if they saw my chest, which has a scar that begins under my left armpit, goes jaggedly across my entire body, and then ends under what

< 126 >

used to be my right armpit. Melody and I call it "the zipper." That's what it looks like, a long red zipper.

Did I, the articulate, militant feminist academic, fail to be the informed, assertive, "new patient"? Or is what happened to me just typical of women's fate at the hands of the cancer establishment? You be the judge. Meanwhile, I'll keep thinking those positive thoughts about Bernie Siegel's "white knights" of chemo and asking myself why I *chose* to get cancer, why so many of my friends *chose* to get AIDS, and we all *choose*, even the most positive-thinking of us, to get...dead. Like they say, don't mourn, organize. Or even better, mourn and organize.

< 127 >

VI

not
surrendering

Rejection
Dragonsani Renteria

SOCIETY REJECTS ME for being Deaf.
The Deaf community reject me for being a Lesbian.
The Lesbian community reject me for not being able to
    hear them.
The Deaf-Lesbian community reject me for being into S&M.
The S&M community reject me for being Deaf.
Society rejects me for being Chicana.
The Hispanic community reject me for being a Lesbian.
The Gay Hispanic community reject me for being Deaf.
Patriarchal society rejects me for being a woman.
I am rejected and oppressed,
Even by those who cry out readily
Against rejection, oppression, and discrimination.
When will it end?

< 131 >

and yet such a small word
Anne-Marie Alonzo

Translated by Lou Nelson

a word, simple word from the heart, word that flows, *agua viva*, wind of shadow or torment, *tempest*, cyclone or cyclops, word that says everything and means nothing (more), word from such a long time ago, island word from a blue country, other country and other century, word stilled, word killed.

there.

a word will not be said. never like that again.

an uneasy girl-child. a woman. nothing else except perhaps the sun of a deep sea. a woman, a child. the mother says: come see Gertrud, we have a visitor. the mother calls. the child hides. makes no noise. is upset. cries. Gertrud wears perfume... Gertrud hugs her and kisses her... Gertrud is old... and... blonde. the child is afraid of blondes. her Arab girlfriends are also afraid of blondes sometimes.

Gertrud is German.

she says: i never gave it another thought, i must have been about five; now i know, only now.

does one pronounce this word for a five-year-old child? if not, at what age, on what day, after the first time or how often must the times be counted?

i, she says, am...

< 132 >

the rest does not come, is begged for, takes on the
impetus of apocalypse *now!* quick, to the doctor,
psychiatrist, psychologist, analyst, i am not ill, she
says again, without saying anything.

and yet such a small word.

silence of the she-lambs.

tell me mother, who am i here?

who? without having every life fall apart, i only want
what is there. because what else is there? on the left or
right, do women say what should be left unsaid?
where is the error? mother.

once upon a time, in an Arab country, a five-year old
child, a blonde German and... the destiny of this life
set.

i, she says sometimes, am different, subversive, look
at my plural lives, look at my credentials — am woman
immigrant disabled poet publisher and... — only one
word will not be written. this text is wanted this
way. without. but with. since un-said and un-
written, and yet this small word writes this text, does
it and undoes it, shows it, assembles it, constructs it without
deconstructing what must not be said.

and yet this small word could it — still — be a danger
for she who rolls it on her tongue before taking it in
her fingers, touching it, taking it out of her mouth,
licking it so that it glistens, sucking it, biting into
it before offering it in secret? could this word cause
harm like that?

i, she says again, am what you see.

*whom do you really see or do you see anyone in the form
of a ...?*

sow, hind, doe, vixen, mare, lioness, flier, ewe, cow, dam,
jenny, roe, nanny, she-monkey, hen, bitch and all those
females whose female names i do not know.

she says: i am also that.

< 134 >

I Am Your Sister
Mary Frances Platt

I am your sister,
but I can't get on the stage to read my words.

I am your sister,
but I go in a door separate from you.

I am your sister,
sitting alone
in the wheelchair only section of the auditorium.

I am your sister,
The abusive bullying infiltrator of lesbian culture,
who finds it
hard
painful
anger making
to sit here and talk with you,
about the violence of inaccessibility,
when I am still not allowed full access
to our conferences,
our celebrations
our culture.

I am your sister,
I am your sister,
I am your sister.

I am your   still   segregated   sister.

< 135 >

Indomitable Spirits Unbroken
Two Feathers

"Do you have an account with us?" she asks.
"No," I reply.
"Sorry, I'm unable to cash your cheque here," is her
unwelcome statement.

Dejected, humiliated.
Blatant discriminative policies everywhere.
"You on family benefits?" they ask in racist voices,
while they look me up and down.
"Ahem, would you like me to drop my pants?" I question.
"Nothing sexual, just look at my scarred knees."
"'Course you can't see the pain in my knees and in my
back too."
"'Course you don't see or hear me
when I have incest flashbacks, deep in the night."

Everywhere I go,
the tools of colonialism — racism,
homophobia, sexism, and classism debilitate me.
Not because I'm afraid of you,
it's my rage.
I'm so tired of parading pain for you to believe.
The negative "isms" and physical pains won't leave me
alone.
Barter, anyone?
I'll trade you for employment.
What did you say?
Did you say no?
Well, I'll give you free advice.
Doesn't cost anything.
Since you're not willing to die in my place,
don't call me lazy Indian (your
term, not mine)
stop telling me how to live my precious life.

< 136 >

Ahem, more free advice.
I do have feelings like other humans.
I'm a strong, 2-spirited Onkwe hon: we
who will survive your
condescending attacks
on my indomitable spirits.

< 137 >

Mae Still Be Alive
Mary Frances Platt

In memory of May Roe

A disabled dyke I know took her life just the other day.
Most say, "Just as well, I could never live like that, a
vegetable you know."
"I'd rather die than lose
an arm
a leg
a fill-in-the-blank."
I say it was a life.
A life taken over by systemic ableism.
Systemic who?
Ableism.   You know.   Or maybe you don't.
All the barriers Mae came across while trying to live
with depression and despair over less functioning everything.
Medicaid pending, rickety electric chair, too few friends,
not enough funding for PAs*

Mae, I honour your life and the choosing of your death.
I remember chicken dinners over girlfriends lost, class
based fights,
mutual early sobriety caffeine adoration, and butch-femme
dreams.
And thanks for the constant supply of Wrigley's gum
when I stopped smoking in '82.
I'll keep up the anti-ableism work, more fuel for the fire.
And although I understand your choice to leave a difficult
body behind
I know that if we as women knew how to live
interdependently now
and if with-holding of life sustaining services for people
with disabilities
were abhorred for the genocide it is,
You Mae still be alive.

* Personal Assistants

< 138 >

VII

testifying

Muscle Fetish
Aspen

A dyke said to me,
"don't you love it when those
                tasty women athletes
all pumping blood and oxygen
power through
some personal hurdle?"

I love it
when my friend asks me to comb her hair
so her strength is free to paint
intricate visions just for herself.

I love it when she sings
taking minute gasps of air between
each tiny sound, cascades of melody
so light they're almost gone
before they reach my ears.

I love it when her worn-out, pressured
muscles, trembling with the onslaught
of a workout she never chose, the burn
which seldom stops, feel a hiatus
which allows her to move and dance.

Dykes dribble over the muscles of dykes
                who walk the hills
                who mend cars
                who dance till dawn
but ignore dykes
                who lie all day in bed
                who cannot direct their muscles
                whose muscles tire easily

< 141 >

Patriarchy told us we mustn't have muscles
but when they bowl we don't have to bat...
we can refuse to play cricket.

You lust after muscles
I lust for spirit.
Watch out for the spirit of disabled dykes
you may not be able to take
such strength.

< 142 >

This Ability
Connie Panzarino

Sometimes I get angry
    "unjustifiably?"
when people waste
    their energy
    their healthy bodies
    and their selves
        on trivia.

I feel
    so driven
    with my minimal
strength.
    I try to chip away
bureaucratic mountains
    with plastic
Carvel
    ice cream spoons
while you put tanks
    in parades
and
    muscles
    into bikinis.

< 143 >

Things That I Hear Too Many Times (Speaking of Fear)
Shemaya Mountain Laurel

Don't tell me that you don't know how you'd survive the circumstances of my life, as if you and I are so different in our capacities for survival. Every one of the many times that I explain how I got from there to here I'm a little more tired, a little more worn, wishing people would take a moment, think, answer for themselves the obvious question. One just does it.

Don't tell me that you couldn't survive what I live with, that I am somehow far stronger than you could ever be. We all find our strength, when we need it, or die. Obviously I'm not dead, yet. And yes, I have found strength that I never would have imagined. But the psychic muscle that keeps me pinned, nose to grindstone, is not a choice. We all find our strength, are found by it, or die.

I am not so different from you. I often have no clue how I will get from this day to the next, what the next bridge to the impossible will look like, where to find the simple faith that the next bridge even exists, or that it's worth the effort of trying to find yet another of so many unending bridges. One just does it, a little at a time, finding the strength for one moment and then when that moment is done, finding the strength to meet the next. When times are hard the moments become very short. When times are easier one has the resources to deal with the larger scale. One does become tougher, and wiser about the process, with the amount of practice that comes of living with so much dramatic change. But the process itself is the everyday version, the same version that gets a person through something as simple as a flat tire on the freeway.

< 144 >

I know it's the opposite of your intention, but it belittles the magnitude of this effort when you propose the idea that I began with any more strength than you have right now. I probably didn't. And I often still don't. I am happy to have the accomplishment of my survival acknowledged — but not at the expense of my membership in the very same community with you and everybody else. We are not so different, you and I. Hopefully the kind of disability that has so changed my life will not arrive in yours, but it could. And you would most likely find ways to deal with it that you had never imagined possible. As I have.

When you ask me to join in the idea of our vastly different strengths, in the idea that you could never do what I'm doing, survive what I survive, you ask me to support the assumption that the kind of disability that I live with could never happen to you. And that is exhausting, infuriating, unfair. I struggle to let go of my own denial; supporting yours is far beyond me. If you think, "I would die first, rather than survive what's happening in your life," there is a depth of honesty that is most likely escaping you.

Many people with disabilities, people living through the hardest of changes, think of suicide. Needing to know there are still choices open, feeling overwhelmed at the prospect of survival in this new pattern, it does come up. But most of us do stay. Bit by bit we find out that we are, after all, able to continue. And find joy.

It's likely that your strengths and my own are indeed different, of different kinds and textures; the abilities we bring to survival are undoubtedly varied in the same way. And as in so many other situations, it is possible in this one to acknowledge difference without building in otherness, without getting caught in the many ways we divide ourselves from our fears, forcing the other person to carry their weight. It is not a matter of who has or does not have superhuman strength; it is a matter of who we each are and how we get

< 145 >

where we need to go. That we each have the ability to deal with obstacles that appear insurmountable is far more the rule than anybody wants to believe; we are more the same than we are different, regardless of the individual paths that carry us.

The problem that keeps people from acknowledging our similar strengths and inner resources has little to do with the question of strength itself — the problem is that in acknowledging our similarities on the level of strength, there is no hiding from our similarities overall. There is no hiding from the possibility that anybody, including the person who thinks she couldn't face it, is vulnerable to dramatic life changes, whether disability, illness or any of the many other experiences that can so quickly catapult any person into that category of "other."

There are two different inflections for the statement that begins "I don't know how I would... " One inflection carries all the connotations of "and this is impossible for me," including both admiration for the other person and fear for oneself. Putting those connotations all together contributes to a careful separation of oneself from the person on the other side of the situation. With so many messages jumbled together in one statement, they become a barrier, leaving no room for honest acknowledgement of each of the individual thoughts and feelings involved. As a result, there is no room for discussion that includes each person's responsibility for herself, that acknowledges each person's life, and fears, and successes.

The other inflection of "I don't know how I would..." is narrower, has a more direct meaning, is a statement that implies "I don't know but I could find out." If that second inflection is put as a question, it asks: "What are the things that I would do? What would the process be like?" The second form carries the assumption that, like the person in front of you, you would make an effort and do whatever you

< 146 >

could. It carries the assumption that this kind of dramatic change could happen to you too, and if it did you would then go on to do whatever was next — which is the most that any of us can expect from ourselves or each other. That second inflection includes the recognition of our common ground, and opens the way to discussion of all the rest. It is that one that I want to hear more.

< 147 >

Remedies
Andrea Broc Lowe

When I tell you
I have arthritis

for god's sake
don't give me a knowing nod
and tell me about Aunt Freda
who had to give up bowling
on account of stiffness in her elbow
or how your knee gives you trouble
now and again

don't look at me like that
as though to say   Are you sure?
I know what you're thinking
I seem too young
really
and gosh
I look so healthy.

I've learned something —
this doesn't have an age
but you know
I feel old sometimes
so old and uncertain and scared
and now I think about aging
before my time

don't tell me to try vitamin Q
or hey, you've heard that Diet
can be useful for this
problem.

< 148 >

You can't imagine the things I do
to get at every angle of my life
to fight this mystery
this monster
fight those doctors
fight invisible deterioration
fight
   back tears

You see
this just came at me
sliced my life into little pieces

sometimes all I can do
is lie there and cry
and wait

when that's over
I get up
and set to work again

Listen. Why don't you find out first
from me
before you offer a cure
for something
you know nothing about.

< 149 >

The Queen of Pain
Barbara Ruth

I am the Queen of Pain.
I have experienced more hurt
In more places
More excruciating
More obliterating
More transcendental
Pain
In my body
Than anyone else in the room
Even though
I'm not the oldest womon here.
I've licked my wounds
In body parts
You don't even know you have.
My pain is worse
Geometrically
Algebraically
Astrologically
Astronomically greater
Than any other person who's ever lived.
Never has any sentient being
In this or any other universe
Suffered
As I suffer.
The Buddha's ten thousand sorrows
Are a puff of milkweed
Compared to my
Enduring
Dreadful
Roots.

And the amazing thing is
I manage so well.
I am so artistically evolved

< 150 >

I can make poems from my pain
For your pleasure.
I am so socially adept
I can disguise my pain
For your peace of mind.
I can sit here
In this body
My neurons screaming out
Their aria of agony
And never make a sound.
Or just a little sound
A wince, perhaps,
A furrowing of the brow.
But I won't bother you with it.

I will listen to your stories
Discuss philosophy
Gossip with you
When all I really want to know

Is how I can get MediCal
To pay for the heroin infusion pump
That fantasy I've lusted for
All these many years.

And on the other hand
I can produce the most heart-wrenching moans
I can make you feel so bad for me
I can bring the tears splashing to your nipples
Seduce you with my ornaments of hurt.

Yes, it's true,
Admit it now, you've heard the evidence.
You must concede
I've won my crown
I *am* the Queen of Pain
Even though, all along, you thought that it was you.

< 151 >

Oxygenated Babe
Mary Frances Platt

Now that I'm using oxygen
I imagine you won't desire me
tube wrapped round breast covering mound belly
over full thighs down long strong foot
trailing over bedclothes sleeze-clothes cunts
wrapping cinching full behind

Now that I'm using oxygen
You probably won't want me
to remove the cannula from my nose
wet your nipple
play tunes with continuous
cool pure air
lick your pussy and share breath
one for me one for you
You probably wouldn't be interested
in hearing a longer louder come
from a stronger safer heart

Now that I'm using oxygen
I imagine you're no longer interested
in spanking mountainous buttocks
renewed sighs of pleasure
moans of release
wrapped in spiralling tubing incandescence
I imagine you wouldn't delight in knowing
lungs are safe for piercing screams
from probing fist
Up and down in and out
now joy and not no breath
which is different than
OH BABY you leave me breathless or
SWEETHEART the sight of you in those tight jeans takes
my breath away

< 152 >

Now that I'm using oxygen
I'd delight in being used
to fulfill any oxygenated babe fantasies
that might be swimming around that
nasty little head of yours
The same head
that refuses to equate severely disabled
with Honey you couldn't possibly make me wet
Cuz I do, and we are, hot for each other

Now that I'm using oxygen
I know I'm still alive feel your touch, touch you
want your body your body wants me
hands tongues cunt-hairs entwined
amidst umbilical cord life-sustaining rhythms

< 153 >

Which map is not whose territory?
Vicky D'Auost

Who Am I?

Not in order of significance, I am a Deaf lesbian mother from a Métis heritage with disabilities who has a Deaf Jamaican daughter; I was a career student and am now employed as a researcher; I have experience as a teacher, community advocate, and writer; I have spent recent years in transition from health to illness to disability. There are many details about these labels which are not self-evident. I have not always been Deaf and have several disabilities which are new as well as a few which have progressed; my daughter was adopted 10 years ago and I have only been working full time for a year. Naming these experiences, which are all a part of who I am, short of an autobiography, helps me to present myself to the unknown reader in categories commonly understood (misunderstood?). Nonetheless, I am still me.

The map is not the territory, the name is not the thing, my (your) labels are not me.

The map is not the territory. The name is not the thing. I have been aware of the socio- psycho-linguistic implications of naming things for many years. A table is a structure that is used for supporting materials above a floor but there is nothing intrinsic requiring it to be called a "t a b l e." In many cultures, the concept of naming has deceived people into thinking the map (which is the representation of the thing) is the territory (the thing). Although some cultures credit names with mystical and real powers, this is not the topic I plan to examine. I acknowledge that all language, written, drawn, signed, spoken or otherwise conveyed has power in and of itself. But I still believe that the map is not the territory. I am not what people label me to be. I am me.

I know that my sense of self includes many names or maps. Some of these I chose but others were applied to me without my permission. I think that many people are harmed

< 154 >

by being categorized by others in negative ways. The maps that have affected me include: not being a real woman if you are a lesbian or if you have a disability, not being a real lesbian if you have children, not being a real minority if you are mixed race, or not having a real disability if it is invisible. I want to look at the impact of maps and conflicts among names or categories but I do not want to evoke pity about people (including myself) who experience multiple maps and experiences. My opinion on maps is that their importance to others has a significant impact on my life and the lives of others who are mapped.

When I was coming out as a lesbian I was not aware of the multitude of possible names which are attached to sexual behaviour or sexual identity. What I knew was that I felt attracted to women, a certain type of women actually. The name "lesbian" was only a formality. Dyke, bulldyke, top, bottom, vanilla, butch, femme, separatist, bi-sexual, monogamous, and other terms became part of my vocabulary and understanding soon after I found lesbian fiction and non-fiction. Similarly when in university I found theories that named what I had been thinking and helped to map my understanding of the world.

During this coming to consciousness of the possibilities of interpreting the world around me, using existing language and theories (maps) and my own response to them, I also became involved in the disability community. As a closeted lesbian, very young feminist academic and a woman who experienced a sudden onset of deafness (lost my hearing) at age 12, I struggled for membership in and identification with many largely unmapped communities. My search for community, for identity and selfhood was largely structured around what names and maps I could find. Although, like all young people, I had some sense that the world was ordered before I joined it, I was deeply disappointed that the world did not revolve around my map.

In university I used the maps which others had drawn to find a sense of self. Some of the maps felt like they did not describe my experiences, yet others fit perfectly. The more

< 155 >

maps I found the closer I thought I was getting to the real name for what I was living. I became more involved with Deaf culture and more involved with the women's movement, and more involved in disability politics. Although I participated in various groups I did not have any group which mapped my entire territory. I was not out as a lesbian with Deaf people and not out as a disabled person (I was Deaf not disabled) with the women's movement. When I graduated I left the country in search of a different territory, and new maps.

I went to work at a deaf school in Jamaica. There I lived as a non-Black Deaf adult teacher in an institution where almost all the staff were hearing and Black and all the children were Deaf and Black. I did have considerable contact with tourists while visiting the beach on weekends, but during the week I lived exclusively on campus in a rural mountain area. My contact with tourists was both frustrating and rewarding. I wanted and needed information from the Americans or Canadians who travelled to Jamaica but I was embarrassed by their behaviour. They were explicitly racist and sexually exploitative of the Jamaicans. To the tourists I was an ally, because they saw me as white; to the Jamaicans I was a foreigner, because they saw me as white, and Deaf. In Jamaica I learned that no matter how I identify myself to me (a Deaf lesbian or otherwise) the names which others call me affect the way they treat me. If men think I am straight, some will probably try to pick me up; if lesbians think I am straight, they probably won't. If hearing people think I am hearing, they generally do not understand my need to lip read; if Deaf people think I am hearing, they disbelieve my Deafness because of my good speech. If people think I am white, they treat me worse or better (depending on their map of what white means). I also learned that race is really about colour. If people think you don't look white, then you are not (to them) white. If they think you look white, then you are (to them). As a mixed race Native/French person this was strangely informative because I had often based race on language and identity but

< 156 >

not so much on colour. In Jamaica I came to understand that many people do use colour of skin as the first and sometimes ultimate test of race.

Names or maps are not only used for race, gender and disability. I found that through interaction with both Jamaicans and tourists my experience with others was largely defined by what people expected me to be. If people thought I was bright or stupid, they treated me accordingly. So, I can be any number of things to myself but my interaction with the world is controlled more by the intersubjective naming of me by others.

I thought that I understood that naming was more important to people than the thing itself. Perhaps this was my first brush with the social construction of reality. I thought that I could apply this new knowledge to my life when I returned to Canada and to university. I felt a new sense of identity formation. I participated actively in lesbian and feminist organizations, out for the first time in Canada. I then found out that my deafness seemed to be problematic to them as much as their hearingness was problematic to me. To compensate I continued to socialize almost exclusively with Deaf people who signed; however, my experience, (being late deafened and attending a hearing university) was not entirely compatible with theirs. I continued my activism with students with disabilities and often served as a bridge between the disabled and deaf communities on committee and in board roles. At this same time I adopted my daughter, as a single lesbian student, and found new maps in that area too. I also became ill with the first of a long series of debilitating problems. Depression came next.

Although my experience of being a Deaf lesbian mother was problematic in that my Deaf friends were not aware of my lesbianism, my partner (for part of the time) was hearing, and my lesbian friends were not generally mothers or even child-friendly; nothing, no map, could have prepared me for the descent into the experience of disability which followed my depression. I became very ill and my experience of life changed dramatically. What was even more dramatic how-

< 157 >

ever, was how people treated me, or mistreated me, on the basis of their naming of my condition. I got better treatment when I had an allergic reaction or an attack of vomiting than when I was suicidal or anxious. I was sympathized with or supported by friends or seen as personality disordered by physicians. My experience of illness and subsequent disability was mapped by others to name what they wanted to understand my experience to be. But the map is not the territory.

I moved to a new city to start again, fleeing from both the maps and the territory. In my new home I found that my new identity was named by people who saw me as I was to them without ever knowing who I was before. I use a scooter or a wheelchair but can walk with a cane. This mobility impairment has only been part of my life for a few years but the new friends I made assumed it was either congenital or long-term. Lesbians who knew me assumed I was and always had been "out" when I was not even out myself! Deaf people did not know I was Deaf long before I was disabled and no one knew about my long-term status as a student or professional but assigned me the new map of "sick." This new map excuses you from work, school, family obligations and life in general. I do not wish to devalue the support I received from all these people who met me for the first time. I received support in the form of friendship, child care, physical and financial assistance, encouragement, and communication. I do not want to imply that these people were wrong to make assumptions about me, because they did so based on what they could see — their maps.

But their maps are not my territory. As a newly disabled person in a new community my sense of identity, my master map, was thrown off entirely by the fact that who I am was not who people named me to be.

There are perhaps only a handful of people who have known me throughout this experience, from pre-Deafness, pre-coming out, pre-motherhood, and pre-disability, to now who can attest to my transformation. But I experienced myself in all the territories and felt an ongoing conflict

< 158 >

between the presentation of my self, my maps, as mother, lesbian, Deaf, disabled Metis, student, professional, etc. But I am not the map and the map is not me.

As a member of various minority communities I know that naming comes from within as well as from the "other". In the community of people with disabilities, which I fondly refer to now as crips, there are clear hierarchies about which people are crip enough. Legitimate disabilities and legitimate policies are determined by the elected or self-appointed leaders of the movement. As a Deaf woman with visual, physical, psychiatric and respiratory disabilities, one might think I would rank pretty high, but I don't. Having severe allergies to perfumes, gases, foods, preservatives and chemical substances is still very much on the margin of the disability movement, despite the fact that it caused most of my other disabilities. As a Deaf woman, who can talk and lip-read, I am not nearly as credible as a quadriplegic and having visual problems which glasses and special lighting can accommodate don't seem to rank recognition. My psychiatric disability is usually left unmentioned and my experience as a woman with multiple functional limitations is named by others who see me as what they do. I have still not come to terms with the possibility that all of my disabilities are permanent or may be progressive so I accept some of the trepidation that others may feel about my membership in cripdom. In the same way, only a small portion of crips understand and acknowledge who I am as a lesbian mother with a mixed race heritage who yearns for academic satisfaction. The naming, and privileging of those named, is part of defining membership, agenda and politics. In order for me to participate I have to at least name myself a person with a disability, and promote the concept that my disabilities and experiences with my disabilities are legitimate.

Similarly in the lesbian community there are lines, clear and not so clear between those who are in the community (out) and those who are not members. Women who have slept with men, or still do, women who never slept with men, lesbians of colour, white lesbians, transgendered, lesbian

< 159 >

mothers, single lesbians, non-mothers, separatists, queers and the butch-femme dialogue are all names used to map the territory of lesbians in and out of the community. As a disabled, Deaf mother who is a lesbian I find it difficult to know where I am; and even looking at the map doesn't help. I have found my experiences, my territory, being challenged by what others see as undeniably objective evidence that I am "out." But their definition of my outness is not me. I know that I am not out to most people, even if lesbians think I look out. Their map is not my territory. To complicate matters, most lesbian events, though not all, are inaccessible to me in my wheelchair, inaccessible because sign interpreters are expensive and not provided, and inaccessible because women wear perfume, cologne or hair spray. I am either made to feel eternally grateful for the sacrifices made to pay for two hours of interpreting for me as the only Deaf woman there, or made to feel extremely guilty for having the nerve to dictate personal hygiene or cosmetic preference to lesbians. I have yet to be at an event or organizational meeting where cross-racial families — meaning my race and my daughters race — have been addressed in the lesbian community. I do not expect that the lesbian community can or will meet all my needs, but I have felt limited by the maps offered to me, maps which do not include my territories.

Another community which I am still an active member of has a process of inclusion to determine who members are and what rank they deserve. I have likened this in the past to an inverted hierarchy of the values of speech and hearing. Hearing people give the highest value to people with excellent speech and hearing and lower value to those without any hearing or speech. In the Deaf community, the naming process, or mapping, values the most Deaf over the least Deaf. Deaf people with Deaf parents, and grandparents, are the heart of the community; Deaf people who attend Deaf schools carry on tradition; Deaf people who can attend regular schools or use their speech are only members if they sign well enough to communicate with the more capital D Deaf people. People who are hard-of-hearing or who are late

< 160 >

deafened are able to participate in roles of mediator or interpreter because they can still communicate well with hearing people, but are never fully accepted into the Deaf community unless they drop their speech. The most recent controversy and a true example of how naming can define the territory are those people who have had cochlear implants. Hearing medical professionals and many parents consider these people a modern miracle and claim they will have the most advantages in life while Deaf people often consider them traitors and have likened the implants to genocide. In this community of Deaf people, which my daughter and I are regular and active members, my status as a parent of a Deaf child puts me on a higher status than my own hearing loss. Because of my education, my English and my speech, I am considered by some to be a "hearing thinker," signed as though I am hearing in my head. Deaf people name my experience to explain my non-Deaf behaviours. Hearing people, too think I am hearing if I do not self-identify as being Deaf. One of the more interesting events that happened to me as a result of being in regular contact with hearing people, is that I have learned most hearing people do not know they are haring. They know they are male or female, white or black but "hearing" is not an attribute they use, unless they have a parent or sibling or friend who is Deaf. Most people who are hearing who meet me realize that much of our differences can be attributed to my Deafness, and after prompting from me, to their own hearingness. From the Deaf, heterosexual perspective, however, the center is "Deaf" and the mother, lesbian, disability, and other names are peripheral. Their map is not my territory and my territory is not well mapped by them.

In Deaf culture however, the hearing person is considered an outsider, as are disabled people, medical professionals and lesbians. There are gay and lesbian Deaf people everywhere but there is still homophobia in the Deaf community. Most gay and lesbian interpreters and Deaf people socialize together in solidarity and there I have found a comfortable map which seems to fit my territory. From my perspective I

< 161 >

see my "being" as named by others in far more ways than my own naming of my life. I am only one person, and although I have some control over my thoughts, actions, and language use, the multiple experiences, roles and contacts I have ensure that the maps made by others about my territory outweigh my self-naming. I suspect that no one in this world has complete control over their identity because we live in a social, technical, ecological world constructed by interaction with others, the environment, animals and other organisms and technology. Given that this suspicion is supported by my experiences of being named by others, I have learned to live with the mapping imposed on my experiences. I could choose to rebel against the mapping by acting in contradictory ways or swimming upstream. I can choose to do both, at different times, or in different environments. But the water continues to flow downstream and despite my own initiative to create my map as my own identity, the world's view of my life affects me on a daily basis.

Social services, training programs, universities, grocery stores, jobs, child care, dances, political organizations, libraries, and even intimate relationships are structured around created maps. As we enter into an experience with these institutions or situations we almost inevitably are assigned or select a name. The name allows us eligibility or disallows us membership and the names are already constructed and pre-assigned by a system not of our making. We become: clients, trainees, students, consumers, workers, parents, partners, members, readers, and lovers, but also people of colour, welfare mothers, unemployable, liberals and queers, all as functions of the naming process. I do realize that our human nature needs a system of processing and organizing all the millions of pieces of data. I know why we name our vegetables and call round shapes "circles" and attach morphemes to our pets and children. Naming helps us to understand the complexities of the world, talk about them and organize our interactions or reactions to the non-self world.

The conflicts then are multiple: the conflict between my

< 162 >

own name and maps of my self which do not always seem to fit my territories or my other maps; the conflict between my map and someone else's map; and the conflict between the multiple maps that other people use to name me or to name my maps. I can only try to be clear about what I map internally, and what I project externally. I know that by using my own maps and naming these maps to the outside world that people who meet me will accept and maybe understand my territories and how they are mapped by language.

The territories then, for me and for others, are spacial, metaphorical, and social. They exist for me and are mapped out by me and by those who watch, interact or speak about territories. But the territories, singular or plural, will remain the territories despite the multiple mappings. I do believe the territories change over time, mine certainly did, but they changed before or in spite of the maps not because of them. We do share many experiences on a social, physical and linguistic level and thus our names and mappings may overall, interact and be reflexive. We can name ourselves, and we can map our territories. But the name is still not the thing. We are still we. I am still me.

< 163 >

Poster Kids No More
Jane Field

```
  E                                    A
They thought we'd keep on smiling for years to come
  E                                    A
They thought we'd just be helpless and mild
   E                              A
Without our own opinion they could just cash in on
  E                         B
Their image of the crippled child.
```

Refrain:

```
   E                          A
But Timmy and Tammy are rebelling
   E                             A
Their Easter seals have come unglued
   E                        A
They won't be apathetic; they refuse to look pathetic
  B                         E
They're changing their point of view.
     A                B
They're poster kids no more,
    E             A   (B, E)
Poster kids no more!
```

(Last time, repeat: Poster kids no more!)

Throw away those images of yesterday
They don't reflect our lives today
Don't tug at the heartstrings; that's not a smart thing
That's not the enlightened way.

It's time to change these ancient attitudes
And show the world a thing or two
If you've got a disability, it's just a different way to be
And you can be proud of it too!

< 164 >

Now the poster kids are living life in their own way
They're everywhere doing it all, (aside: And some of us
are lesbians!)
You'll find us in real life, not in a still life
Not with our backs to the wall.

(Title: Thanks to Shelley Tremain)

< 165 >

passing
Sherree Clark

passing for
healthy as in
not using the cane
lifting heavy objects
denying the curve of fingers by
painting the nails bright pink
passing
as in kidney stone
invisible
passing as in
almost failed

passing for fear
of the same response I
got yesterday and the day before that
I've a cousin who's twenty and in a
wheelchair permanently or I know someone
who got it so bad they were bedridden or
the worst you poor poor thing

< 166 >

I pass on that
the newest cure
the best medicine
passing over
as in too disabled
passing on
as in not contagious
as in did I tell you that
I'm not what you'd
expect
accept
except in passing

From the series of poems entitled "Living with Arthritis."

< 167 >

VIII

yearning

Bird Spirit
Allison Sletcher

ink on paper, 12" w x 5" h

< 171 >

And Still I Fight
Kathleen Rockhill

May 1993

It is not so long ago that I was a relatively healthy able-bodied woman. A feminist committed to challenging the hegemony of privilege in defining human rights, I knew all the right words, even had the right sentiments. I cared about access; sometimes I included "differently abled" in the string of qualifiers I attached to the universal concept "woman."

I once had a lover who was less able-bodied than me. I learned to be sensitive to her limits, to her contradictory needs to be independent and cared for. Sometimes I raged with her at the unthinkingness of others. Sometimes I got frustrated with her for not even trying to do things I cared about, like hike or canoe. I took it for granted when she did what I could, never fully appreciating how hard she must have had to push herself to do what I did so easily. Really

I didn't have a clue
All I knew
was that I didn't want to offend, or leave out, or erase or
be insensitive or unsupportive
Most of all ... I wanted to

*do the **right** thing*

I was not able to live with every breath of my body, to see in every photo my eye fell upon, to feel in every eye that nervously shifted its gaze from mine, to sense in every room I entered, to remember in every activity I undertook, to read in every line I read, the reality, the difference, the invisible concrete walled-off boundaries, between the "able-bodied" and those restricted by a society that doesn't give a shit about their presence; a society that doesn't feel the absence of those whose bodies don't conform to the physical demands/assumptions of normalcy.

Mentally, emotionally, I have been the disabled one,

< 172 >

limited by the prerogatives and fears of "the normal" from appreciating the complex worlds of the "differently abled"; ignorant of the riches and poverties that separate out, that denigrate and dismiss, vital lives that I was too ignorant to miss, so framed have I been by the stultifying world of "the normal," the ever-present ever-invasive images that draw me, images that haunt me.

It saddens me greatly to think of this: that we do not *know*, do not feel in my bones the plight of those socially cast aside as "other," until I have lived it. Twice this has happened to me now. First, when I "chose" to identify as a lesbian, and then when I was hurled into the world of disability, not an identity I would choose, given the choice ... and yet ... and yet ...

The arrogant ignorance that privilege nutures

What does this say? What hope does this hold out? Can we ever learn to see, to feel, beyond the walled-off boundaries that privilege builds? To know, to feel so intensely that we cannot forget, what it is like to be cast outside the easy assumptions of privilege, what it is like to be ignored in the wastelands of indifference, to be left in waiting upon the patrons of good intentions?

Like access ... so they put up the blue wheelchair sign... maybe even put in a ramp, or a bar or two (if I can manage to get to the toilet and some able-bodied person hasn't perched herself upon it) ... designate a parking spot where they are sure no able-bodied people will be inconvenienced (if yet another able-bodied person has not chosen to ignore the signs) ... and that means *access* ... (I've yet to see an able-bodied person call the police to report that a designated disabled parking space is blocked. Have you?)

so conscientious, so good they are
I want to **SCREAMMMMMMMMMMMMMMMMMMMMMMM**
Carry a can of red spray paint with me wherever I go
wage guerrilla warfare

< 173 >

I think a lot about privilege, about how to rupture the taken-for-granted *right to be* that accompanies privilege, how to see through the limits of my class and race privilege, how to work with others dedicated to the politically in/correct mantra, working to right the violences of the "isms" of gender, race, class, age, ability, sexuality, ethnicity ...

Maybe the most I can ever hope for is to know that I don't know; to listen, really listen, as if my life depended upon it.

* * *

June 18, 1993

Whoever I am

In memory of Lois Heitner

I must believe
I am not
and will never be
the only
one
who suffers.
        Cherríe Moraga

How could she die? Another statistic. Another fatality on the 401. The agonizing nightmare. No words come to capture her light, her laughter, her intensity, her energy, her determination, her fight. No words to capture the loss to all who knew her, the pain her lover must suffer.

Her spirit haunts me all this week. Ever since that early morning moment when Jaki called:

I am getting ready to make my first drive alone, getting ready to go to Peterborough to begin the terrifying business of replacing the vehicle I crashed; getting ready to do what I am not ready to do, what I am terrified to do, what I must do if I am to continue to live in the country

getting ready to do what I am not ready to do

< 174 >

fear so great the only greater fear I know is to let this fear win
getting ready when the phone rings
Jaki? What's wrong?

**NO! NO! NO! NO! NO! NO! NO! NO! NO! NO! NO! NO!
NOOOOOOOOOOOOOOOOOOOOOOOOOOOO!!!!!!!!!!!!!!!!!**

LOIS? Lois, oh Lois oh lois how can it be i cannot let it
in all night it tears at me i put you away day after day
no one wants to know no one wants to hear no one can
let themselves know the agony no one can go near their
greatest fear there is no room for tears the tears that tear
at my heart the tears that no one wants to see to know
to feel the tears that creep into my restless sleep the tears
that speak what no one wants to hear

* * *

Except Becky. Does she know? Some of the time I feel
like maybe she does. We have lived through it together all
these months death so near it nearly chokes us

and now it's time
                    ready or not
my time is up
Becky has to move on, to live her life
no longer can she be my cushion
hard reality glares

ready or not i must go out into this world alone, learn to
overcome my limits, my fears, learn to accept what I cannot
do while endlessly pushing myself to take yet another step,
to look fear in the eye, to know that I too will die and there
is no way I can control where when or how

*let me never forget the pain I have suffered; let me never forget
that in the hours of my most excruciating agony, I would have
given my life to be where I am now*

< 175 >

When I despair I take out the photos Becky took the day after the accident.

It takes my breath away to see my smashed-up truck, to see the cold collapsed metal, to see the damage to the driver's side, to imagine how I survived, to see the damage to the passenger side, so thankful that I was alone.

It takes my breath away to see the smashed-up carcass
NO
IT IS ME
It is my smashed up body lying there, legs pulled apart, pinned down by the weights of traction. Eyes swollen shut against the pain, bruised puffed-out cheeks, nose in stitches, mouth set in a grimace, blue hospital gown against stark white sheets. White purple red skin stretched over the broken frame of bones conceals the damaged nerves that die within...
ALIEN
Except for that wrist wrapped in hospital bracelets of plastic. Every time I see it tears come to my eyes. So vulnerable. It is set there like a broken bird's wing just above the huge purplish hand that lies listlessly upon the clean cotton sheets.

They tell me I have to look ahead, think positive, not give up hope, not look back, have faith that I will walk again, that everything will be all right. Maybe. I don't think so. "You don't think so now, but everything will be OK. It will be. You can't give up hope. You have to think positively. You'll be just fine. You'll see."
NOT ME
Always when I get scared, when I feel the dull pull of despair, I have to go back to that place of my greatest pain, to remember what life demands I forget. To remember back to that time when I would have given anything to be where I am now, to know again that I want to live, that I can take pleasure in little things, like being able to see the flowers bloom, hear the bird's song, feel the warmth of the sun

< 176 >

against my skin, breathe deep the misty clean air brought by the spring rain.

Sometimes it works. My life in clichés.

A constant balancing act, walking the tightrope between remembering and forgetting

Just to balance, to walk again — to feel the wet grass beneath the soles of my feet, to feel my weight centred low in my limbs, that delicate ecstasy of power charging through the earth, travelling up through my soles, through my calves, through my thighs into my pelvis, gently rocking me to the tune of life's sensuous call

GONE FROM ME.

* * *

July, 1993

How to buy safety? How much does it cost?

I have the privilege of having a choice. Can I buy enough metal to put between me and all that might harm me? Can I buy enough metal to ward off rapists, homophobes, burglars, killers? Can I buy enough metal to overcome my fear? Can I buy enough metal to compensate for my paralysis?

And if I had a gun, would I have enough metal to shoot?

How much does it cost to buy safety?

How much metal do I need to surround me, to protect me
> driving the 401
> limping along the streets of Toronto
> living, partially paralysed, alone in the bush of the
> north country.

I buy exactly the same vehicle as I crashed.

Did its reinforced steel sides and roof save my life? Or did its height tip me to my near death? I torment myself. Finally I choose life. Pat says it takes a lot of courage to buy the same vehicle. Still it takes my breath away. Am I being just plain stupid? Is there any way to predict, to know, to buy, safety?

How much I have to make myself forget. To get behind

< 177 >

the wheel again. To stay alone in the north country. To drive the icy winter roads. To face down my fears.

Each moment I am behind the wheel, I relive the accident; every time I come upon a sharp turn my breath drops through the floor waiting frozen in fear to see if anything's coming at me around the bend. I feel so small so broken now behind the engine's power. What's a middle-aged crippled lady like me doing with such a macho vehicle?

My wheels. My dykemobile. My Black Beauty. My strength. My power.

Each day I hoist my body up onto her lap, get behind her wheel and come a little closer to feeling at ease with her again.

One day I will ride with her again, glide with her over the rolling hills, smoothly turned curves opening out onto the long narrow expanses of breathtaking country roads. I will.

This is new for me, this fear. Always, before, I made myself face fear down. I would hurl myself headlong into the abyss of my fears, yell out to the demons to come get me if this was my time, dare them until they went away. No way they were going to rule my life.

My spirit is broken now.

* * *

August, 1993

I read back through my journals since the accident. The unrelenting pain a memory now.

I flip flop. One day thankful to be alive, the next anguished by my limitations, my losses.

The hospital in Peterborough. Searing pain. Nurses scold me for taking too many pain pills, scoff at my "complaints" of being unable to breathe, of pain caused by the rod rammed into my pelvis. Spasms through my leg jolt my entire

< 178 >

body like bolt upon bolt of lightening. Sleep never comes. There is no escape. Pinned down. Alone. In my raging frustration, I fear I'll hurt myself. On the seventh sleepless night I hire someone to sit with me; she comes for three nights, when, at last, I succumb, for an hour or two, to sleep.

The hospital ordeal lasts for six weeks and one day. A long lonely stay. I am at the mercy of nurses who treat me like a piece of rotten meat. Except for Dorothy, who saves my life one night when she convinces the specialist to check out why my breathing is so laboured ("You almost died twice," she tells me as I'm leaving). Cindy and Linda manually unpack the block of constipated shit that my bowel will not release. A fourth nurse whose name I do not know, sits quietly at my bed for several minutes at a time during the agonizing nights when sleep never comes. I wonder if she is a dyke.

How do you measure homophobia? Is it in the way I am treated — with complete disrespect? In the way they treat Becky, who they ignore day after day as she comes to give me the care they will not give? When she asserts her concern as my partner, she is subjected to seething scorn by the respiratory specialist who threatens not to perform the dangerous procedure he has said is necessary to my life; Bec has had the "audacity" to ask him about his success rate with the operation. He is the *only* choice I have. Furiously, I lick ass; as much and as fast as I can, anything to mollify him to feel safe enough to have him perform the goddamn "procedure." Then there are the nurses who lift my arm and ask one another: "Have you ever seen hair like this under a woman's armpit before?" Day in and day out indignities as they refuse to give me my pain medication, ignore my pain, throw my leg around as though it's a sack of dirty laundry, belittle my needs, laugh at the amount of pills I'm taking. How do you measure homophobia?

Turns out I had pneumonia. Turns out there was a build-up of fluid in my lungs caused by a fractured rib that had punctured the lung's lining. Turns out my pelvis was fractured. Turns out the metal bar of the splint they used for

< 179 >

traction was rammed right into my cracked pelvis. Turns out my fractured femur was "highly unstable." Turns out there was irreparable damage to my sciatic nerve.

Gradually it dawns on me that I will never "get better," that I will be crippled for life. I finally utter those words to Bec, asking how she can live with a cripple, sobbing that it is more than she has bargained for. Bec rocks me in her arms, crying, "don't say that, don't call yourself a cripple." But I am crippled. It's the only word that feels real, the only word that captures the pain I feel, the only word that captures what I must live with, forever.

As I get ready to leave the hospital, terror sets in. I cannot bear to be so dependent on Becky. I've found her mood swings while I am in the hospital frightening. She's scared about my coming home, about all the responsibility it puts on her. I'm terrified beyond all reason of how dependent I am, how trapped I am, unable to care for myself, unable to protect myself. Barely able to move, I am a total burden.

Watching. Weighing. Waiting. In the weeks that follow I struggle with my limits. Ever mindful of Becky's moods, fearful of igniting her anger, I am constantly looking for the right moment to ask, to dare to risk, throwing me back to the terror of my childhood:

what can i ask for? what can i push myself to do? how can i think creatively about meeting my needs? what can i do without?

No matter how I try to spare her, constant work is required of Becky, as she must not only care for me but assume responsibility for all the household chores I once did. The two of us alone up here, Bec is my sole source of contact with the outer world — shopping, doctors, therapists — all my needs fall on her shoulders. She is too exhausted for pleasure. Pleasure becomes synonymous with not having to be responsible for me, or so it seems to me.

Friends urge us to move back to Toronto where we can have more support. We cannot bear to give up our home, our woods, our river. Where would I stay in Toronto? I can't

< 180 >

walk, can't handle stairs. How would we move? Who would do the work? Bec insists she wants to stay.

I feel the heartbeat go out of my home, out of my life. There is no music. There is no movement. There is no warmth. I am confined to the house. I sit two feet away from the stereo I can no longer work. I watch the cold black wood stove that I once used to heat our home go unkindled. I become aware of how I used to be in a state of perpetual motion, especially in the evenings as I rhythmically glided from chopping vegetables, to stoking the fire, to changing the record, moving to the beat of my favourite music, *The Indestructible Beat of Soweto*, volumes 1, 2, 3 and 4, grafted onto my body. Now, it breaks my heart to hear it.

Bec and I are in deep trouble; we are drowning under the weight of my need, our private pains. I am scared by Becky's need to find her pleasure away from me, time when she can feel free of responsibility for me. We bring to our troubled situation, troubled histories, violent pasts that poise us, like the clashing clang of cymbals, in opposition as we dance the tangled dance of taking care of/refusing to erase oneself/in the face of the need of the other. We both want, desperately, to be *seen* by the other.

My mother and grandmother schooled me well to never, under any circumstances, be a burden. Like them, I can not imagine that someone might love me just for who I am. The accident has wiped out any sense of power/value I had: my capacity to care for others, my generosity, my sensuality, my sexuality, even my mind. I can not imagine why Bec would want to be with me. I feel her unhappiness. I am terrified that she will leave, a terror intensified lightyears by the knowledge that I can not live on my own.

I am acutely aware of how my sense of power has been defined sexually. I revelled in feeling the earth's energy rise through the soles of my feet into my pelvis. For many years I had worked to overcome the physical/sexual effects of incest in my body by teaching myself to lower my weight deep into my pelvis, to move with my "cunt open," to feel the power of my legs. When I am first able to stand after the

< 181 >

accident, to begin to bear weight on my paralysed leg, I howl at all I have lost. I am unable to feel anything through the hollowness of my leg, the plastic brace that holds my foot in place.

* * *

January 30th, 1994
Eighteen thousand kilometres on my vehicle since July, travelling from one therapy to another: acupuncture, chiropractor, trager, massage, psychotherapy.
Daily exercise routine of two plus hours, one hour a day on the acupuncture machine, nightly hook-up to the muscle stimulator machine.
getting stronger, oh so slow. my leg shows no signs of regeneration... hobbling around the house like a jack rabbit with a pegged leg.

The bloody exercise bike comes to symbolize how I feel:
Cycling my brains out
                no matter
how hard i work how fast i cycle how much i push myself
I am eternally **stuck** in one place
Silence so deep
                strangulating isolation
SCREAMING my heart out when I cannot bear the silence another moment
GOING NOWHERE
Day in, day out I fight to keep going, not to give up hope in the face of despair

endless	*monotonous*	*battle*
courage	*anguish*	*fear*

I have travelled more in these many months than I have in my lifetime
GOING SOMEWHERE
I have never imagined

< 182 >

Bec and I have made it through
                              so far
Wounds sealed deep beneath details of the every day

I don't know how I'll get by, how I can continue to live
in the country, how I'll manage to work, if I'll be able to
walk or feel the grass under the soles of my feet again.
Layer upon layer of hope gives way to the agony of
acceptance
And still I fight

* * *

November 6, 1995

I resist the urge to wrap it all up; to tell you what has
become of me now, twenty-one months after my last entry,
three years to the day since my accident; to create a linear
narrative with a beginning middle end. I resist the urge to
completion, clear only that, however much I may think I
know where or who I am, and project that stasis onto the
future, I never know what's coming round the bend.

Instead I want to pick up the thread with which I opened
this narrative. The question of privilege. Interesting that this
was my starting place, the subject of my first piece of
reflective writing on the accident. Odd, really odd, as I look
back that that is where I would begin. An academic question.
And yet, it is one that continues to interest and unsettle me.

Compared to other disabled women, I am "privileged,"
both materially and physically. While I am seriously limited
in my ability to walk, I am not confined to a wheelchair or
a scooter; in order to buy a house in downtown Toronto that
could accommodate my physical limits, I had to assume a
huge mortgage, a mortgage I worry about being able to
continue to pay when the auto insurance portion of my
income benefits are cut off today. But I was able to qualify
for the mortgage; I have a lovely home for as long as I can
manage the payments, as long as I can manage it physically.

What is privilege? What does it feel like in the texture of
everyday life? Money counts. A fully functioning body counts.

< 183 >

The power to define "reality," for one's self and others, counts. A presence that is desired by the dominant society counts. Still, the dichotomized hierarchy of either/or, of privileged or not privileged, obscures the contradictory and complex ways in which power works to define im/possibility.

One way in which I understand the terror I have lived since my accident is as a story about my "fall from privilege." This is an overdramatization, but it captures how I've felt. The foundational assumptions upon which my subjectivity was formed were framed through an unarticulated sense of my location in relation to privilege. In some ways I continue to reap the rewards of my accumulated privilege; it is the heritage of that privilege that helps me in my fight. I am highly educated, articulate, know how systems work, do not settle for bureaucratic limits, know how to pursue my rights from decades of having assumed and/or fought for them. When I no longer enjoy the rights I once did, I am outraged. I fight. What has changed is that I rarely win.

When I reflect upon my account, when I feel the fear that envelopes me, when I let despair have its day, it is my "fall from privilege" that I feel so acutely. Physical limits, my inability to accomplish that singular goal of the insurance companies and their endless line of rehab specialists — the goal of full-time work — my refusal to sacrifice the body I have left to that all-important goal, leaves me at the mercy of bureaucrats. They do not respect me as a fighter, they do not care about my well-being; their job is to cut my benefits. I am defined as uncooperative when I resist their plan for me. I worry financially in a way I have not before; there are no other jobs where I can meet the underlying assumption/demand of physical normalcy. I am dependent upon my employers as never before. Who else would hire me? Who wants to accommodate a partial cripple who cannot perform as though not crippled, like the publicly packaged Lucien Bouchard? So I do what Mike Harris says all disabled people should do, work at my old job for half the pay so that I can meet the assumptions of able-bodied standards.

My life is at the mercy of the medical system. Not

< 184 >

physically. There is little that they can do for me. They hold the power of assessment, of defining whether and how much I can work, what benefits I'm eligible for, what therapies I undergo. I now see my choice of doctors as about politics. To get support for non-western therapies, like acupuncture, I must have an approved Western-trained doctor testify to its necessity for my healing. To refuse to see the specialists my insurance company sends me to, or to refuse to engage in the programmes they endorse, is to jeopardize my benefits. My body has been taken over by an endless barrage of medical practitioners, each of whom works on a different piece of me. I long for an advocate, someone on my side, fighting for and with me. Not only am I positioned as a "client" in this system, and an "uncooperative" one at that, but also as one who doesn't want to work, one who will do whatever she can to milk the system.

The subtext, of course, to my being positioned as "unco-operative," is that I neither look like, nor behave as, a "nice white, middle-class, middle-aged lady"; I refuse to/no longer *can* perform myself heterosexually, or camouflage that I'm a dyke.

I become sullen and angry. I do not want to deal with yet another professional where I am asked to repeat the details of my accident and its effects; I am sick and tired of justifying myself, of telling yet another deceptively kind face that "I love my work. I want to work; that's not the problem." It's my body and its inability to conform to the assumptions of your world that's the problem, not my "lack of motivation."

I refuse to be your victim.

Another way in which I feel my "fall from privilege" is in my coinage as a sensual, sexually attractive woman. I am struck by how I learned to perform by body so as to maximize my sexual capital. It's about my pleasure and desire, and it's about how you see me, how your gaze positions me. I work hard to counter the physical "deform-ities" of my body, to look "normal." My gait is getting better, my centre of gravity is gradually shifting from my shoulders downward, but walking with a limp and a cane, a leg that

< 185 >

flails out to the left, is not the way I would choose to perform myself, given the choice.

I have "special needs" now — needs that don't go away. I've come a long way from those early months; still I am seriously limited in what I can do. In the breakup of my relationship, one of my most painful moments was when Becky told me that she had not been able to ask herself whether she stayed with me out of love or out of her inability to abandon me in my need. I am thankful that she stayed during my hardest time; I do not know how I could have gotten by without all that she did for me — *and* it's a soul destroying way to be loved. It's true, there was little space for her pain, for how her life was radically interrupted and turned upside down, *and* she was free to walk; eventually she did. Becky and I are not alone in this struggle with the "burden" of another's needs. Power in relationships radically inverted in that "fall from privilege."

To be sure, I'm still privileged. While I'd give almost anything to have my legs/my body back, it sure is easier being paralysed with financial resources than without.

I don't want your pity.

I am troubled by this concept of privilege. I want to stop attaching privilege to individuals, as though it's a state of being or a commodity that one does or does not have, and to think instead of acts, of what it is that one can do, in varying situations, and in relation to whom. Privilege is about power, the power to effect the actions of others, the power to exert some control over one's life, to know the possibility of choice and rights that are inscribed by 'the normal'. Power is about having value, that is, skills, abilities, performances, that effect possibility for others, that others desire. We learn to perform ourselves in ways that will maximize our power to realize our desires. That these desires are socially constituted matters. Who desires to be disabled? Who desires to be around disabled people? We are socially organized out of society. Our absence is not missed. Because the disabled are pitied, defined as tragic, a burden to society, our insights and capacities are not prized — they are not even recognized.

< 186 >

Since my accident I may be a "better person," even a "better worker," but what I have to offer is not what counts in a society possessed by the production of "the normal," the material idealization of bodies and achievements.

* * *

March, 1996
I see little choice
now
I fight for my life
up against
webs of callous indifference
webs spun of
the arrogant ignorance
that privilege nurtures.

Exhausted
this tired body
breaks down.

Tired of fighting ...

I think a lot about the politics of "disability." What does it mean when those of us with vulnerable physical resources, most with severely restricted economic resources, are left to fight "our own" battles? Or when we are left in waiting upon the patrons of good intentions, who do not exactly see the plight of "disabled dykes," or queers, as their rallying call? What will it take for lesbians, gay men, queers of all colours and classes, to see that our politic cannot be limited to our sexuality? To see that our bodies, our desires, our differing "needs" and the various discriminations we must face day in and day out, are intensified by, at the same time as they transcend, our sexual preferences and practices?

< 187 >

Rain Woman
Rhianon Ca-thro

I have a vision
of raining women
tear dropped
body parts
suspended in space
separate
in forced isolation
in chosen seclusion

I have a vision
of raining women
tear dropped
body parts
that hold knowledge
of illness
suspended in space
separate
in forced isolation
in chosen seclusion

I have this vision
of raining women
tear dropped
body parts
suspended in grief
separate
in forced pain
in chosen anger

< 188 >

I have a vision
of raining women
tear dropped
body parts
coming together
in healing
in voice
in stories
as survivors
of illness

body parts suspended
speaking their memory
their story
their knowledge
of healing

I have a vision
of rain
healing drops
falling on women
who have supported me
in my experience of illness
through their own relationships
with illness.

< 189 >

Hospital Green: The Psych Ward
Pauline Rankin

They take your clothes
and lock them up

re-issue you
in hospital green

you merge
as a swaying

drooping
pacing
sea

In this place
there are:
1) Clothes People
2) Pyjama People

there are cool rooms
flat/steel/blue/grey
(I am a pyjama person)
walls have fallen
colours swirl
I have paper feet

I glide by
in clean hospital green
of a depressed ghost
unseen by clothes people

They talk about "the patients"
"the wife" "the job" "the stuff"
I am not supposed to understand
but
I once had clothes too

< 190 >

I have not yet learned to vanish
my sponge ears soak in their words

At first I tread water
then float
then crawl
in my sea of hospital green
each stroke gets stronger
soon I will swim away

< 191 >

Survival, Silence and the Obvious Remains
Frances Yip Hoi

Translating silence across productive incapacity
disordered moods fall deep into despair
traversing moments of relentless action
manic thoughts
that you follow with your tongue
repeating words that collide with such accidental rhythm
followed by silence

When I am unable to meet your demands
with sentences unformed to inform and disclose
in panic
unspoken experiences of thoughts in collision
spoken across word
imagined through image
in fragmentation
visions of excess and decay
in fermentation
opportunity seized by terror and panic
and caressed by fantasies and dreaming
in memory
there are moments
bedridden by composure
silence
and the obvious remains

Panic
materialized during moments of
unpredictable hysteria
losing sense of time as moments pass
breathing conflates with chasms of breathlessness
asthma, bronchitis, fear of choking, environmental responses
dry mouth

< 192 >

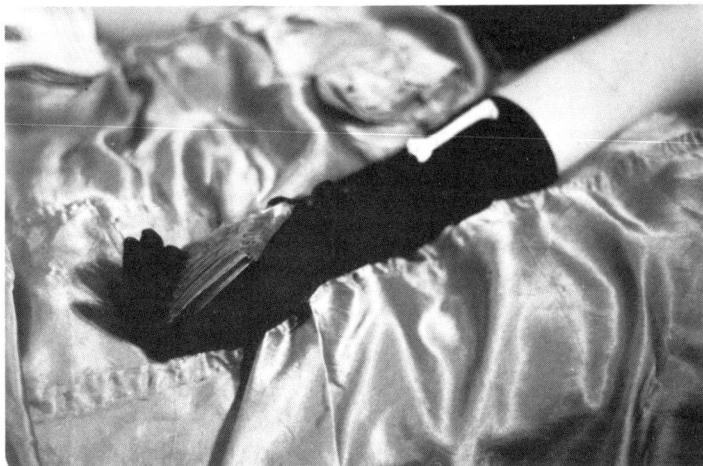

echoed by visions of composure
as I am unable to whisper the words of defeat
when I cannot live up to your expectations
in between manic and depression

Memories of victory and defeat
in repetition
my voice resonates across the limitations
of silence
and the meanings
of the words I use
that try to explain and nearly reduce through
explanation and illusion
bodies of knowledge, experience and memory
in witnessing, reading and re-telling
stories of survival

Crusades
across my mind
as the battlefield
in ritualistic medical treatment
in the naming and conquest
of disordered moods
manufactured consent

< 193 >

are strategies and invocations
in the marketing of
salvation and recovery
through pharmaceutical
consumption

Prozac, Tofranil, Paxil
anti-depressants to induce daily excitation
valium to tranquillize at the site of exile
mind altering my reality
Lithium to stabilize moods
of loss, trauma, anxiety
beyond all physical signs
only the obvious remains
are the scars that mark
reconstructive knee surgery
scars that recall
memories of physical violation
moments of silence

Moments of endless tears
tearing deep
in between memory and memory extinction
returning from shock treatment
moments spoken about her return home

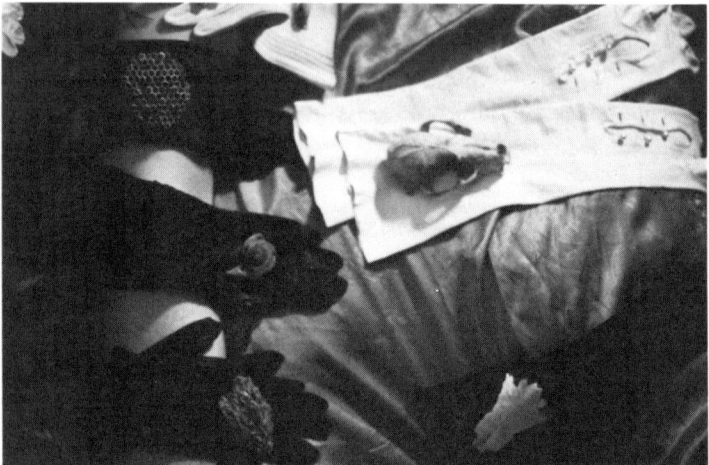

< 194 >

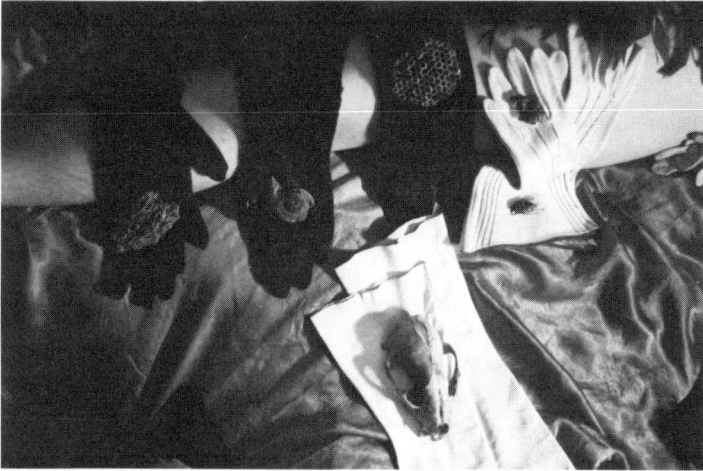

to be with children that she had not seen in years
immobilized by feelings, experiences, alienation
relationships
as lovers, friends and family
in exile
interrupted by years of drug therapy and tranquillizer
addiction
identity transformation
in the selling of fantasies
new and improved personalities
purchased at the expense of
memory loss
residing at the moment of silence
at the moment in between hope and despair

Unspoken
are the experiences
hospitalized and drugged
restrained
and considered to be incapable of making decisions
losing the right to vote
and lack of privacy
during institutionalization

< 195 >

marked
before I open my mouth
labelled
as unstable
incapable
disabled
emotionally handicapped
irrational
manic/depressive

Frantic
thoughts of my disembodied self
unmaterialized except in memory
beyond the flesh
beyond the scars
healing across silence

Attempting suicide
is a symptom of depression
in an all girls' Catholic school
at confession
thoughts of women loving women
are received with silence
and prayers for redemption are spoken
in between moments of absence
abstinence
and absolution

Translating silence as resistance
in psychiatric recovery
as fears of aversion therapy
increase panic attacks
in between moments of
incapacity and productivity
where thoughts of loving her are
heard louder
than prayers for guidance and recovery
when silence is encouraged

< 196 >

to preserve illusions of normalcy
in between sacred and profane
when I choose silence
in order to maintain the safety of distance
in situations of privilege
when silence is an informed decision for self preservation
disclosure about illness is often received with discomfort
and guarded responses

Ecliptic visions of
victory and defeat are imagined
when I photograph
images that preserve and detail
manic depression
as a form of resistance
when certain women are misdiagnosed
marginalized
by limits of normalcy
and hierarchies of privilege

exiled
as other, abnormal, different
excluded
only to witness
difference
as social decomposition
composure as ideal
and translating silence
and the obvious remains
as evidence of survival

< 197 >

Homeless
Barbara Ruth

When I say I was homeless
I mean
That my home was pesticided
That I had to leave
That I couldn't come back
That sick and scared, I scrambled
From place to place
From one friend's house
To another
And never felt at home.

When I say I was homeless
I don't mean
That I lived in a shelter
Or in a car
Or on the street
Or in a nursing home
Or on a psych ward
Or in jail.

My friends
Worked for hours, for months
To keep me safely homeless
Or safer homeless
Or as safe as it could get.

I was scrambling
No time to grieve my losses
I was busy
Suing people
Being sued
Hustling
To find the next place

< 198 >

Keep my welfare trip together
No time
To consider
My spiritual welfare
No time to decide
What to make time for.

Being EI and homeless
Meant my oxygen company cut off my air
Because I moved around too much.
Being EI and on Section 8
Meant I got kicked off because I didn't give 30 days notice
Before leaving my poisoned subsidized house.

Being visually impaired and EI and busy with lawsuits
Meant I had to hire attendants
To enlarge all the paperwork
So I could read what I signed.

Being homeless and unable to walk
Meant I was prepared to give up environmental safety
For a place wheelchair accessible.

Being poisoned and sick and homeless
Meant giving up the luxury
Of a private place to throw up.

Being homeless and epileptic
Meant fighting with people I stayed with
And coming to on the floor
With them helping me get into bed.

Being epileptic and seizing out of control
Meant trying to deal with meds
I called the pharmacist and said,
"I'm taking Dilantin and Klonapin
And Phenobarbitol and Valium.
How far apart should I space them?"

He asked why I was awake.
I didn't know
The answer.

Being epileptic and seizing out of control
Meant learning useful facts
About my body and drugs
— If I ever decide
To push my wheelchair across the US
To make a political statement
I'm sure Dilantin would get me there.

Having seizures and drugs and pesticides scrambling my brain
I was righteous
And angry
And scared
Of what I might do.
All things considered
I didn't do bad.

Having EI and epilepsy
And chronic hepatitis and multiple sclerosis
And being homeless
And trying to keep my SSI
My IHSS
Get back my Section 8
Deal with attendants in three counties
And people I might stay with in five
Keep records for lawyers
And doctors
And social workers
And everyone
Who wanted,
Who needed to know
What really, really
Was going on...

< 200 >

I think I fucked up
I focused on the wrong things,
Didn't know
Who I was supposed to tell what.
I was homeless and
Trying to keep a story going
Trying to find some humour in it
— I was scrambling
To stay in the category
Of people who tell funny stories.
Sometimes I got the facts wrong.

I was too much and I knew it.
I could have, should have
Done better.
I got caught up in a whirlwind
And was scrambling to stay right-side up.
All things considered, I did a hell of a job.

But truly, I lost it,
Between seizures and ketones and
Raging all over the place
I lost it
        And got it together.

My friends gave me good advice.
They were mostly sick and disabled themselves
They gave what they could and sometimes more,
My friends put me up
And I was a lot to put up with.
There wasn't an end point to all this catastrophe
No one could think of a happy ending
My friends tried to make it
So wherever I landed
Wasn't the end of me.
I wound up in a hospital. I don't know
If I wanted to go there or not.
"Want" was a country

< 201 >

That wouldn't give me a visa.
I thought I might commit some revolutionary act
So at least I could feel some pride
Then wait to be hauled off to jail
So at least I could fight with my jailors
Instead of my friends.
I thought I might live on the land
At Point Reyes National Seashore
Dodging the rangers as long as I could
Enduring the elements as long as I could
So at least I'd get some fresh air and beauty.

No one could think of a happy ending.
Everyone planned and replanned, and then I got caught
    in a fire
And then I got caught in a hospital
From there things got worse
And better.

For four months I was homeless.
I stayed in 10 places,
Was mean to people who didn't deserve it.
Lost my clothes, my possessions,
Ninety pounds
Of my flesh...

I was homeless.
And desperate   And dearly loved.
And, damaged,
I did come through.

< 202 >

Lockout
Jade

Weeping her heart out,
Feeling of anger, depression and fear
There are five walls around her,
No way to any opening,
Somewhere lost in soul, hoping
One day someone will guide her out
From the ordeal of walls around her.

Struggling to push down walls...
    She fails.
Screaming her lungs out for help,
    No one hears.
Pounding on the walls...
    No one opens.

Weakening ... can't push anymore ... ready to die...

The key ... to the opening
Will lead her out of rages.
There's got to be a clue
To her being alive ...
Until one day she found the key

    and

Reached out in touch with herself.

    Free...

at last ... she lives.

< 203 >

Connections
Judith Moses

At 13, she walks behind her mother, never once actually looking at the rounded, humped back ahead of her. With adolescent desperateness, she hopes that no one will know, or even suspect, that she is related to this tiny, deformed woman. At 25, she watches with horror as her own shoulder blade slowly flares, lifted away from her body by a spine which is curving steadily to the right. She knows the scoliosis was coded into her body long before her birth; yet she is certain that this is her punishment for that day, years ago, when she abandoned and ridiculed her mother. She is grateful that the "corrective" shoes, the "corrective" surgery, the endless exercises and the ballet classes she was forced to endure as a child now allow her to wear regular shoes, providing they have an ankle strap; her sister and mother are limited to children's running shoes and Tender Tootsies. She doesn't know why the women in her family all "have trouble with their feet" — there is mystery and shame surrounding their difference — and although no one has explicitly said so, she knows that she must never mention their "problem."

At 30, she adds CMT and "neuromuscular disorder" to the growing list of labels she uses to describe her differences; although the mystery has been solved, the shame remains. As she struggles to reclaim and accept her body, the label survivor, one of the most painful she has woven into her identity as an adult, becomes increasingly textured. At 33, she returns to orthopaedic shoes, sells her standard car and begins a daily ritual of strapping her legs into knee-high braces. She is pleased that she can manoeuvre herself through familiar surroundings without her two canes; she is grateful she can still manage a few stairs. Every night, she lifts her legs out of their plastic casings, and with a tenderness that belies her rage, she checks her feet for open sores and rotting skin. As she pulls the sheets over her wasted legs, she struggles with the relief she feels that she is not yet a

< 204 >

permanent wheelchair user; acknowledging her own ableism proves to be one of the hardest challenges she must face.

In the quietest corner of her mind, where logic has no place, she wonders why she is being punished this way. And in the stillness that is her pain, she wonders if he did this to her when he pushed and pulled, twisted and tore, at her small self — is it possible that he somehow broke or damaged her in such a way that she is now unable to stand on her own two feet? Rational thought reasserts itself and she knows this is absurd; still, she struggles to understand why, for most of her life, she has been so hated. The answer emerges as she comes to understand that she lives in a world which tells her that, as a woman, she is worth nothing; as a lesbian, she is worth less than nothing; and as an aging, disabled lesbian, she is losing ground every day. Balanced against these judgements is the power and privilege she is granted because she has white skin, a university education and a christian heritage; her life becomes an intricate dance as she struggles to reconcile these conflicting realities.

She remembers something a beloved friend once said to her: "This is life. This is it. How many years do want to practise before you take the risk to actually live it?" So, with a strength she has come to trust as truly her own, she harnesses her rage and learns to honour her grief. She embraces the women in her family, accepts the genetic load, separates her abuse from her disability, and chooses to truly live in the body which has served her so well; she digs deep, touches her courage and "she" becomes "I."

< 205 >

Seizure
Aspen

Swimming in thin consciousness
my body still walks
as I jolt to reality
further down the street,
my eyes are open but don't see
fast cars pass me
my automaton legs follow
my lover as I lose touch
then flash back briefly
in a garden. Far away
I see her words forming
loving eyes concerned
knowing I will leave her
when the priestess
takes hold
violently
wrenching the body
shaking with transition
shocking entry
into the cave
of fierce dreams
with a future and past
colour and sound
memory and thought
belonging and knowing
time stretched
to a lifetime...

the grip is loosened
awareness seeps back
my lover's caring face
as she tells me her name
and I ask her mine.

< 206 >

She holds me, body and mind
bruised, I lose that other place
completely, strands of meaning
shrinking away. She tells me
where I am and how long
I've been gone — minutes
only it seems, for worlds
to shine
and burn out.

I struggle for understanding
to give me back
a place in gritty reality
seeking intimate knowledge
from her eyes.

< 207 >

IX

reinscribing

Melody Heartbeat of a Black Deaf Woman
Jade

I am a black deaf woman
With a character of harmony
The music of my songs
Silence to my hearings
But visual to my world
Listen to my melodies
Beneath my flapping wings...
I hear no tunes...
I put my hand on my chest
Just to feel the heart beating...

I am a proud deaf black woman
The music of my song
Who plays the tune
By singing with my hands
Moving, animated in the air
To your dear heart

So powerful is the name of my song,
I can be seen signing hummings
Through the night breeze
I hear no tunes
Just feeling my heart beating...

< 211 >

A Virtual Harvest

Lisa Comeau

there's a small basket of green apples
a language, silent
growing inside me

turning colour, multiplying, swelling
heavy as gossip
there are many
can you hear the talk talk talk?

crab apples materialize
they pop out of my mouth,
squeeze out through my ears
do you hear a rumour?

wherever i go they fall,
dropping on the floor of the laundromat,
rolling under waiting room tables,
sliding into my shirt
cold and smooth

now some come out of the top of my head
with a cartoon pop pop sound
and spring out
into the winter air
crisp

some rot inside, festering and waiting
growing curious forms of fungus
not yet defined

< 212 >

Saturday at the Farmer's Market
a virtual harvest emerged,
exploded, immobilized me —
a cash crop!
a small child in Osh Kosh
clapped gleefully
as if i were a new toy
a Christmas mall display
her worried parents
grabbed her arm
pulled her away

Sunday in my kitchen
talking with a short-haired friend
the apples were wild
possessed
engaged in violent debate
one hit her in the eye
she left early

others are raging hot glowing
like candy apples
just shrink enough
to squeeze out through my pores
then grow big again
on the outside

they've even begun to edge out of my vagina
winesaps, wet and bulb-like
crowding into my jeans

   "Dr. Gawd will see you now."

   "Hello get undressed put this on
   get up on the table lie down
   put your feet in these."

< 213 >

The stirrups have knitted
covers with faces. Dr. Gawd clamps my cunt
to the table with cold metal,
talks about skiing and the Red Sox,
sticks a gloved finger in, pushes on
a spot above my bladder with the
other hand.

I stare at ceiling tiles, mobiles,
diagrams of the reproductive system.
He smells like antibacterial soap.

"Everything seems okay. Have you been
under stress lately? Didn't you say
you were a single parent?"

sometimes they get into the lungs
drop in with thick pulmonary thump sounds
herding, whispering

but the ones that frighten
are the ones that stick
whole and round
in my windpipe
stretch it
almost rip it
suffocate me
my tongue dangles
uncontrollably
no warning
things become dry
the panic of no air
of no mouth
blue-faced
i want a new language

< 214 >

"Hello, I'm Dr. Smith
what can I do for you?"

"I feel like I'm going crazy.
I can't get out of bed. I get
sick whenever I go outside."

"How's your appetite?
How's your energy level?
How much sleep do you get a night?
Are you restless?
Are you unable to make decisions?
Do you feel like hurting yourself?
Do you spend a lot of time daydreaming?
Do you cry often?
Do you feel like you're in a fog?"

"I eat a lot. I am always tired.
I sleep ten hours a night and
yes yes yes and..........yes."

"It seems you are clinically depressed.
It's not your fault, it's probably a
chemical imbalance. I'm going to prescribe
Elavil. Take one a day and come back
in two weeks."

"I don't like drugs."

"If you don't want to cooperate
then there's no point in you
coming back. Now, do you want to get
better or not? It's up to you."

such a common food
so breeding and parasitic

< 215 >

i walk the sidewalks and worry
can you see the fruit in my throat?
can you see how my neck protrudes?
i can't lie anymore

the apples come out of my skull now
and make my hair fall out
like hay

handfuls of crackly hair
stick to my sweater

"Hi I'm Dr. Wesson."

"Hello."

"So, tell me about your symptoms."

"Well...I've been having dizzy spells
and balance problems, my face goes numb
on one side, my speech slurs and my ears
ring."

"Okay. Sit up here."

He taps spots on my arms and legs
with a rubber hammer.
Then rolls a pointy star on my legs.

"Can you feel this? And this? Stand up
put your arms out close your eyes
hmm...take a few steps forward."

His eyebrows crunch together.
His thin lips are pasty dry.

< 216 >

"I see nothing at all wrong with you.
It's quite common for all of the symptoms
you've described to be caused by anxiety.
You should try deep breathing exercises."

my hands now look foreign to me
white, delicate, and false
suited to ticket — taking
carnivals, ring — wearing

apples the size of walnuts
burst out from under fake nails
like goblins

today i had errands to do
walked with borrowed legs
step crunch step crunch

you could smell the cold
sharp and blue
chimney smoke
vertical and hushed
exhaust fumes and breath
congealing, suspended
things are too clear
even the edges of my dress
are cutting

at the bank
they squeezed out again
convulsed
rolled all over the marble floor

an old woman
talcum powder hair
coughed discreetly
glared
tellers nudged other tellers
eyes opened like tent flaps

< 217 >

oh please don't let this happen today
i don't want this to happen today
how long can i hold it together
hold on hold on i gotta i gotta
hold on i think and think and think

i ran out into the busy street
to make my way home
pedestrians tripped on them.
cars flattened them
i edged behind a corinthian column
flew through an alley way
hopped on a bus

oh just hold on we're nearly there
stop stop please stop
keep quiet until we get out of here
this is not how i want to be known
oh no you can't take over
you must stop so stop

i hold my bulging coat together
muffle the apples
some roll over the bus floor
like billiards

tonight while i sleep
the apples are chaos
gravenstein, macintosh,
golden delicious
speaking secret dialects
in the morning they rest
all around my bed
in quiet piles
obedient   and tired

< 218 >

Aknoha
Two Feathers

Verse I

Oh, Aknoha, you worked so hard for survival,
cleanin' white folks homes for two dollars a day.
Walkin' six miles down that dusty road,
with blistered feet.

Chorus

Oh mama, I know you hear me,
callin' out your name in my restless sleep.
I know you wouldn't want me to give it up.
Be strong you always said, keep it up, keep it up.

Verse II

Oh, Aknoha, you fought so long,
against racist hatred.
I never thought you'd die the way you did.
Since you went to the spirit world, I'm hurtin'.

(Chorus)

Verse III

Oh mama, you were so strong.
A beautiful woman, a fine teacher.
I'm walking in your footprints, the matriarchal way.

< 219 >

(Chorus)

Verse IV

Oh, my spirit is cryin',
but I'm from strong people.
Survivors and resisters.
No one can hold our spirits down.

(Chorus)

Verse V

I'm livin' in a racist town,
fightin' every night and day.
Strugglin' for all oppressed people.
Standin' strong against the white power, yes I am.

(Chorus)

(Extro to chorus)

Oh, Aknoha, I know, I know, you wouldn't want me to give it up.
Be strong you always said, keep it up, keep it up.

< 220 >

Clay Woman
Rhianon Ca-thro

dedicated to Iman

I write
because it soothes
no medication
no drug
no addiction
soothes like the rhythm
of words
in my head
spewed out on a page
no medical system
        new age
           healing hoax
              shit ass
                  sales pitch
                      on my health
                          as a commodity

loosens the phlegm
soothes raw tissue
eases food down
through snake spirals
coiled pain
knotted memory
history
of my body
of the medical system
in illness

< 221 >

my illness in words
in writing
voiced as a tool for healing
so that one day
illness
may not be a word
and my body
one with myself
not splayed open

              on a page
              a medical document
              an examination table
              a test
              a diploma
              a certificate

not scattered in parts
              on a bed
              in a bar
              on the job
              in politics

so that one day \ my body \ may be \ one \ with myself

< 222 >

Post-mastectomy Fantasy
Louise Lander

I would bloom lilies on my scar,
sprout gay balloons on my deflated chest,
revive what has been battered down.
The void is not just physical —
there is a subtle loss as well
of energy, chi, prana, life force, some
important something that was there, got lost
between the table and the microscope.
But maybe if I chant, burn incense, breathe
a special way, do something magical,
it will return, find life anew on flattened chest,
create an aura where there is no substance,
make strength out of a wound.

< 223 >

Passages from *A Burst of Light*
Audre Lorde

April 20, 1986
St. Croix

Blanchie's birthday. When Blanchie had her mastectomy last year, it was the first time that I had to face, in a woman I loved, feelings and fears I had faced within my own self, but never dealt with externally. Now I had to speak to these feelings in some way that was meaningful and urgent in the name of my love. Somehow I had known for the past eight years that someday it would be this way, that personal salvation of whatever kind is never *just* personal.

I talked with Blanchie today over the phone about this feeling I have that I must rally everything I know, made alive and immediate with the fire of what is.

I have always been haunted by the fear of not being able to reach the women I am closest to, of not being able to make available to the women I love most dearly what I can make available to so many others. The women in my family, my closest friends. If what I know to be true cannot be of use to them, can it ever have been said to be true at all? On the other hand, that lays a terrible burden on all of us concerned, doesn't it?

It is a matter of learning languages, or of learning to use them with precision to do what needs to be done with them, and it is the Blanchie in myself to whom I need to speak with such urgency. It's one of the great things friends are for each other when you've been very close for a long time.

And of course cancer is political — look at how many of our comrades have died of it during the last ten years! As warriors, our job is to actively and consciously survive it for as long as possible, remembering that in order to win, the aggressor must conquer, but the resisters need only survive. Our battle is to define survival in ways that are acceptable

< 224 >

and nourishing to us, meaning with substance and style. Substance. Our work. Style. True to ourselves.

What would it be like to be living in a place where the pursuit of definition within this crucial part of our lives was not circumscribed and fractionalized by the economics of disease in america? Here the first consideration concerning cancer is not what does this mean in my living, but how much is this going to cost?

November 6, 1986
New York City

Black mother goddess, salt dragon of chaos, Seboulisa, Mawu. Attend me, hold me in your muscular flowering arms, protect me from throwing any part of myself away.

Women who have asked me to set these stories down are asking me for my air to breathe, to use in their future, are courting me back to my life as a warrior. Some offer me their bodies, some their enduring patience, some a separate fire, and still others, only a naked need whose face is all too familiar. It is the need to give voice to the complexities of living with cancer, outside of the tissue-thin assurance that they "got it all," or that the changes we have wrought in our lives will insure that cancer never reoccurs. And it is a need to give voice to living with cancer outside of that numbing acceptance of death as a resignation waiting after fury and before despair.

There is nothing I cannot use somehow in my living and my work, even if I would never have chosen it on my own, even if I am livid with fury at having to choose. Not only did nobody ever say it would be easy, nobody ever said what faces the challenges would wear. The point is to do as much as I can of what I came to do before they nickel and dime me to death.

Racism. Cancer. In both cases, to win the aggressor must conquer, but the resisters need only survive. How do I define that survival and on whose terms?

So I feel a sense of triumph as I pick up my pen and say

< 225 >

yes I am going to write again from the world of cancer and with a different perspective — that of living with cancer in an intimate daily relationship. Yes, I'm going to say plainly, six years after my mastectomy, in spite of drastically altered patterns of eating and living, and in spite of my self-conscious living and increased self-empowerment, and in spite of my deepening commitment to using myself in the service of what I believe, and in spite of all my positive expectations to the contrary, I have been diagnosed as having cancer of the liver, metastasized from breast cancer.

This fact does not make my last six years of work any less vital or important or necessary. The accuracy of that diagnosis has become less important than how I use the life I have.

December 15, 1986
New York City

To acknowledge privilege is the first step in making it available for wider use. Each of us is blessed in some particular way, whether we recognize our blessings or not. And each one of us, somewhere in our lives, must clear a space within that blessing where she can call upon whatever resources are available to her in the name of something that must be done.

I have been very blessed in my life. I have been blessed to believe passionately, to love deeply, and to be able to work out of those loves and beliefs. Accidents of privilege allowed me to gain information about holistic/biological medicine and their approach to cancers, and that information has helped keep me alive, along with my original gut feeling that said, *Stay out of my body.* For me, living and the use of that living are inseparable, and I have a responsibility to put that privilege and that life to use.

For me, living fully means living with maximum access to my experience and power, loving, and doing work in which I believe. It means writing my poems, telling my stories, and speaking out of my most urgent concerns and against the many forms of anti-life surrounding us.

< 226 >

I wish to live whatever life I have as fully and as sweetly as possible, rather than refocus that life solely upon extending it for some unspecified time. I consider this a political decision as well as a life-saving one, and it is a decision that I am fortunate to be able to make.

If one Black woman I do not know gains hope and strength from my story, then it has been worth the difficulty of telling.

< 227 >

Other Cultural Work of Interest to Disabled Dykes

BOOKS

Anthologies

Browne, Susan E., Debra Connors, and Nanci Stern, eds. *With The Power of Each Breath: A Disabled Women's Anthology*. Pittsburgh and San Francisco: Cleis Press, 1985.

Elwin, Rosamund, and Karen X. Tulchinsky, eds. *Tangled Sheets: Stories & Poems of Lesbian Lust*. Toronto: Women's Press, 1995.

Elwin, Rosamund, Dionne Falconer, Mona Oikawa, and Ann Decter, eds. *Out Rage: Dykes and Bis Resist Homophobia*. Toronto: Women's Press, 1993.

Keith, Lois, ed. *Musn't Grumble: Writing By Disabled Women*. London: The Women's Press, 1994.

Luczak, Raymond, ed. *Eyes of Desire: A Deaf Gay and Lesbian Reader*. Boston: Alyson Publications, 1993.

Nestle, Joan, ed. *The Persistent Desire: A Femme-Butch Reader*. Boston: Alyson Publications, 1992.

Rudd, Adrien, and Darien Taylor, eds. *Positive Women: Voices of Women Living with AIDS*. Toronto: Second Story Press, 1992.

Sang, Barbara, et al., eds. *Lesbians at Mid-Life: The Creative Transition*. San Francisco: Spinster's Book Co., 1991.

Saxton, Marsha, and Florence Howe, eds. *With Wings: An Anthology of Literature By and About Women with Disabilities*. New York: The Feminist Press at the City University of New York, 1987.

Silvera, Makeda, ed. *Piece of My Heart: A Lesbian of Colour Anthology*. Toronto: Sister Vision Press, 1991.

Warland, Betsy, ed. *Inversions: Writing by Dykes, Queers, & Lesbians*. Vancouver: Press Gang Publishers, 1991.

Fiction

Makino, Erika B. *Six of Cups: A Circle of Stories*. Redwood Valley, CA: Earth Books, 1992. To order a copy, send $8.50 US (postage incl.) to: Earth Books, P.O. Box 740, Redwood Valley, CA 95470.

< 229 >

Autobiographical Narratives & Reflections

Brant, Beth. *Writing as Witness*. Toronto: Women's Press, 1994.

Butler, Sandra, with Barbara Rosenblum. *Cancer in Two Voices*. San Francisco: Spinsters Book Co., 1991.

Lorde, Audre. *A Burst of Light*. Ithaca, NY: Firebrand Books, 1988; Toronto: Women's Press, 1992.

------. *The Cancer Journals*. San Francisco: Spinster's Ink, 1980.

Millett, Kate. *The Loony-Bin Trip*. Don Mills: General Publishing, 1990.

Panzarino, Connie. *The Me in the Mirror*. Seattle: Seal Press, 1994.

Thompson, Karen, with Julie Andrzejewski. *Why Can't Sharon Kowalski Come Home?* San Francisco: Spinsters/ Aunt Lute, 1988.

Poetry

Alonzo, Anne-Marie. *Lead Blues*. Translated by William Donoghue. Montréal: Guernica, 1990.

Ruth, Barbara. *Past, Present & Future Passions*. Santa Cruz, CA: Her Books, 1986. To obtain a copy, write: Her Books, P.O. Box 7467, Santa Cruz, CA, 94061.

Non-fiction

Gillespie-Sells, Kath, and David Ruebain. *Out-Disability*. London: Channel 4 Television, 1992. Produced by Broadcasting Support Services to accompany the video *Double the Trouble, Twice the Fun*. To obtain copies, send SASE (self-addressed stamped envelope) to: REGARD, Disabled L & G Group, B M REGARD, London, England, WC1 3XX.

Loulan, Jo Ann. *The Lesbian Erotic Dance: Butch, Femme, Androgyny, and Other Rhythms*. San Francisco: Spinster's Book Co., 1990.

Morris, Jenny, ed. *Able Lives: Women's Experience of Paralysis*. London: The Women's Press, 1989.

Oikawa, Mona, Dionne Falconer, and Ann Decter, eds. *Resist: Essays Against a Homophobic Culture*. Toronto: Women's Press, 1994.

< 230 >

Stone, Sharon Dale, ed. *Lesbians in Canada*. Toronto: Between the Lines, 1990.

Tremain, Shelley, ed. *Bodies of Knowledge: Critical Perspectives on Disablement & Disabled Women*. Toronto: Women's Press, forthcoming.

SPECIAL ISSUES OF JOURNALS

Canadian Woman Studies/les cahiers de la femme. "Women and Disability." Vol. 13, no. 4 (Summer 1993).

off our backs. "Issue on Disability." Vol. 11, no. 5 (1981).

Sinister Wisdom. "On Disability." 39 (Winter 1989/90).

ARTICLES

Browne, Susan E. "Infusing Blues." In *With the Power of Each Breath: A Disabled Women's Anthology*, edited by Susan E. Browne, Debra Connors, and Nanci Stern. Pittsburgh and San Francisco: Cleis Press, 1985.

Chartrand, Lina. "Centre Stage: Life as Little Miss Easter Seals." In *On Women Healthsharing*, edited by Enakshi Dua, Maureen FitzGerald, Linda Gardner, Darien Taylor, and Lisa Wyndels. Toronto: Women's Press, 1994.

Connors, Debra. "Disability, Sexism, and the Social Order." In *With the Power of Each Breath: A Disabled Women's Anthology*, edited by Susan E. Browne, Debra Connors, and Nanci Stern. Pittsburgh and San Francisco: Cleis Press, 1985.

Disabled Lesbian Alliance. "Open Statement from Disabled Lesbian Alliance." *off our backs* vol. 11, no. 5 (1981).

Doucette, Joanne. "Redefining Difference: Disabled Lesbians Resist." In *Lesbians in Canada*, edited by Sharon Dale Stone. Toronto: Between the Lines, 1990.

Field, Jane. "Coming Out of Two Closets." *Canadian Woman Studies/les cahiers de la femme* vol. 23, no. 4 (Summer 1993).

Folayan, Ayofemi Stowe. "It is a Very Good Year." In *Lesbians at Mid-Life: The Creative Transition*, edited by Barbara Sang, et al. San Francisco: Spinster's Book Co., 1991.

Gwidzak, L. "Disabled Lesbian Tells Her Story: No Longer Alone." *Gay Community News* vol. 12, no. 6 (March 1983).

< 231 >

Hearn, Kirsten. "A Woman's Right to Cruise." *Trouble and Strife* no. 9 (1986).

Hershey, Laura. "Pride." *The Disability Rag* (July/August 1991).

Koolish, L. "Coalition Building: Disability Caucus." *Perspectives* no. 5 (1986). Reprinted in *Sinister Wisdom* 39 (Winter 1989/90).

Lloyd, Betty-Ann. "No Longer Silently Disabled." *Healthsharing* vol. 4, no. 8 (Fall 1987).

Martindale, Kathleen. "Can I Get a Witness? My Lesbian Breast Cancer Story." *Fireweed: A Feminist Quarterly of Writing, Politics, Art & Culture* no. 42 (Winter 1994).

Masur, Judith, Jessica Barshay, and Ruth Atkin. "Love and Tsuris." *Bridges: A Journal for Jewish Feminists and our Friends.* vol. 3, no. 1, (Spring/Summer 1992).

Mudd, K. "Disability, Race and Gender." *off our backs* vol. 17 (August - September 1987).

Nestle, Joan. "N.Y. Lesbian Illness Support Group: What Being a Lesbian Means in the Deepest Sense." *off our backs* vol. 11, no. 5 (1981).

Phoenix, Val C. "Breaking Through Denial: HIV-Positive Lesbians." *San Francisco Bay Times*, December 5, 1991. Reprinted in *Community AIDS Treatment Information Exchange* (CATIE) HIV-Positive Women Information Package 20, June 1992.

Rotenberg, Lorie. "Winning the Battle: Living with Epstein-Barr Virus." In *On Women Healthsharing*, edited by Enakshi Dua, Maureen FitzGerald, Linda Gardner, Darien Taylor, and Lisa Wyndels. Toronto: Women's Press, 1994.

Sager, J. "Five Reasons Why I Play Wheelchair Basketball." In *With the Power of Each Breath*, edited by Susan E. Browne, Debra Connors, and Nanci Stern. Pittsburgh and San Francisco: Cleis Press, 1985.

------. "Hanging Out with Disabled Lesbians." *off our backs* vol. 11, no. 5 (1981).

Tremain, Shelley. "Coming Out as Disabled Dykes." *Quota* (February 1993).

------. "Creating Our Own Images." In *Peeling Off the Labels: Women, Sexuality, & Disability.* Toronto: DAWN Toronto, 1992.

< 232 >

Waite, Rosie. "They Didn't Know What To Say To Me." *Gossip: A Journal of Lesbian Feminist Ethics* no. 1 (1986).

Zackre, Sheila. "On Disability: Language and Meaning." *off our backs* vol. 15, no. 1 (1985).

MAGAZINES AND NEWSLETTERS

CTN Magazine. National glossy magazine for Deaf lesbians and gay men. Published three times per year by Dragonsani Renteria. For subscription information, send SASE to: CTN MAGAZINE, P.O. Box 14431, San Francisco, CA 94114; (415) 626-9033 (TTY/Fax).

Deaf Queer Resource Center. Electronic Magazine (free). DQRC@hooked.net (Internet); http://www.deafqueer.org (on the Web).

Disability Rag, The. Published by Avocado Press. Includes articles on ableism, violence against disabled persons, and disability culture. Regularly features news items about UK and US chapters of ADAPT, a direct-action organization of anti-ableist activists. To subscribe, write: THE DISABILITY RAG, Box 145, Louisville, KY 40201 USA. Available in various formats.

Dykes, Disability, and Stuff. Quarterly newsletter by and for disabled dykes. Published since the early eighties. Features writing, reviews, and calls for submissions. To subscribe, write: D. D. S., P.O. Box 8773, Madison, WI, 53708 USA. Available in various formats.

HIKANÉ: The Capable Womon. Disabled Wimmins Magazine for Lesbians and our Wimmin Friends. Consistently inspiring publication. Features narratives, reviews, and illustrations, by and for disabled dykes. Includes bulletin board. Produced, edited, and published by Jodi. To subscribe, write Jodi at: HIKANÉ: The Capable Womon, P.O. Box 841, Great Barrington, MA 01230 USA. Available in various formats.

Mouth: The Voice of Disability Rights. Radical US news magazine which focuses especially on ableism inflicted upon those who have experienced brain-injuries, and on the struggles of disabled persons incarcerated in rehabilitation hospitals and nursing homes. For

< 233 >

subscriptions, write: MOUTH, 61 Brighton Street, Rochester, NY, 14606 USA. Available in various formats.

Our History. Newsletter published by the National Deaf Lesbian, Gay, & Bisexual Archives. For subscription information, send SASE to: The National Deaf Lesbian, Gay, & Bisexual Archives, P.O. Box 14431, San Francisco, CA 94114.

PHOTOGRAPHY

Boffin, Tessa, and Jean Fraser, eds. *Stolen Glances: Lesbians Take Photographs.* London: Pandora Press, 1991.

Boffin, Tessa, and Sunil Gupta, eds. *Ecstatic Antibodies: Resisting the AIDS Mythology.* London: River Orams Press, 1990.

Hevey, David. *The Creatures that Time Forgot: Photography and Disability Imagery.* London and New York: Routledge, 1992.

Spence, Jo. *Cultural Sniping: The Art of Transgression.* London and New York: Routledge, 1995.

VIDEOS

A Prayer Before Birth (1992). Dir. & prod. by Jacqui Duckworth. Drama based on the director's own experiences with multiple sclerosis. Chronicles the physical and emotional journey of an African American disabled lesbian. "Simultaneously desperate and defiant." Distributed by Women Make Movies, 462 Broadway Ave., 5th Floor, New York, NY, USA; (212) 925-0606 (voice); (212) 925-2052 (fax).

AnOther Love Story: Women & AIDS (1990). Dir. & prod. by Debbie Douglas and Gabriella Micallef. Dispels myths around HIV and AIDS for lesbians in particular and women in general. By focusing on an interracial lesbian relationship, one member of which might be HIV positive, this video provides insight into the ways in which various communities, particularly the Caribbean community, contend with issues surrounding sero-positivity. Distributed by V-TAPE, 401 Richmond Avenue, Suite 452, Toronto, ON, CANADA M5V 3A8; (416) 351-1317 (voice); (416) 351-1509 (fax).

< 234 >

Cutting the Edge of a Free Bird (1992). Dir. & prod. by Jade. A Deaf African American lesbian wants to attend a hearing university rather than Gallaudet. She struggles to find a way to tell her Deaf mother that this is so. Also depicts the Deaf dyke's relationship with a hearing lesbian. American sign-language interpreted, and with sub-titles. Distributed by Jade Films, Inc./Deafvision Filmworks, Inc., 232 West 114th Street, New York, NY, 10026 USA; call 1 (800) 421-1220 for relay operator to (212) 666-0648; (212) 932-0861 (fax & voice).

Double the Trouble, Twice the Fun (1992). Dir. by Pratibha Parmar. Prod. by Parmar in cooperation with REGARD, a British organization of disabled lesbians and gay men. Interviews with disabled lesbians and gay men who sign and speak about ableism within lesbian and gay communities, lesbo/homophobia in disability organizations, access, identity, isolation, and sexuality. British sign-language interpreted, and with sub-titles. Distributed by V-TAPE, 401 Richmond Avenue, Suite 452, Toronto, ON, CANADA M5V 3A8; (416) 351-1317 (voice); (416) 351-1509 (fax).

Positive Images: Portraits of Women with Disabilities (1989). Dir. & prod. by Julie Harrison and Harilyn Rousso. Designed to produce positive realistic representations of the lives of disabled women and the social, economic, and political issues that they face. Offers crucially needed role models for disabled girls. Sub-titled. Distributed by Women Make Movies, 462 Broadway Ave., 5th Floor, New York, NY, USA; (212) 925-0606 (voice); (212) 925-2052 (fax).

Toward Intimacy (1992). Prod. by The National Film Board of Canada in co-operation with DAWN Canada. Focuses on the lives of four disabled women: a white oral Deaf lesbian, a straight Métis woman, and two straight white women. The four women discuss relationships, sexuality, sexual abuse, and identity. Sub-titled. Distributed by The National Film Board of Canada (NFB), 150 John St., Toronto, ON, CANADA M5V 3C3; (416) 973-9110 (voice); (416) 954-2698 (fax).

Voices Heard, Sisters Unseen (1995). Dir. & prod. by Grace Poore. Focuses on the experiences of marginalized

< 235 >

survivors of domestic abuse (for example, Deaf women, lesbians, immigrant women), women for whom the currently available social support services are inadequate. Sub-titled. Distributed by Women Make Movies, 462 Broadway Ave., 5th Floor, New York, NY, USA; (212) 925-0606 (voice); (212) 925-2052 (fax).

Voices of Positive Women (1992). Dir. by Darien Taylor. Prod. by Michael Balser. Examines the impact of HIV and AIDS on the lives of women. Nine women give personal accounts of the inadequacy of services for HIV+ women, the compounded effects of racism and HIV on women of colour, sexuality for HIV+ women, and how they have transformed isolation into activism. Distributed by V-TAPE, 401 Richmond Ave., Suite 452, Toronto, ON, CANADA M5V 3A8; (416) 351-1317 (voice); (416) 351-1509 (fax).

MUSIC

The Fishing Is Free. Written and performed by Jane Field. Songs about being disabled, lesbian/gay self-defense, and more. Available on cassette. To obtain a copy, send $10 Can. (postage incl.) to: 111 Belsize Dr., Toronto, ON, CANADA M4S 1L3, or send $10 Can. to W.R.P.M., 517 College Street, Suite 232, Toronto, Ontario, Canada M6G 4A2.

A Double Shot of Sherry. All songs written by Sherry Shute. Performed by Shute with others. Includes the song "Lost in The Swamp." Available on cassette. Send $7.50 Can. (Can. postage incl.) to: Sherry Shute, 305 Melita Ave., Toronto, ON, CANADA M6G 3X1. Available in the US from Goldenrod Distribution, (517) 484-1712 (voice).

< 236 >

Contributors

Anne-Marie Alonzo is a poet, fiction-writer, playwright, editor/publisher and literary critic. She was born in Alexandria, Egypt on December 13, 1951, and has lived in Quebec since 1963. To date, she has written twenty books, among them *Lead Blues*, which won the Emile-Nelligan Prize in 1985. She has taught creative writing at the University of Montréal and her work has appeared in numerous anthologies and reviews in Europe, Quebec, the United States and Canada. Co-founder and co-director of TROIS, a review and a publishing house, in 1987 she also launched AMA Productions, a company which produces books-on-cassette.

Aspen is a political disabled lesbian passionate about life, love, friendship and positive change. She is a contributor on disability, lesbian and feminist issues to a variety of publications in the UK and USA. Aspen has worked in factories and a petrol station, as a painter and decorator, playgroup assistant and eventually a teacher. She's taught creative writing and done some editing. Aspen has been writing all her life but long-term illness has seriously affected her output. Her poems have been published since the 70s, read on Radio and TV and used in theatre productions. She's had many short stories published and is hoping to find a publisher for her novel about disability. She hopes other disabled women will write about their lives and that non-disabled people will find a cure for their often chronically negative attitudes towards disabled people.

Rhianon Ca-thro: After five years of pharmaceutical treatment as a youth, the repercussions of medical experimentation have stayed with Rhianon Ca-thro's body well into her twenty-seventh year. Despite medical labels attached to her disability, Rhianon considers her disability to be the medical system and an illness of that system which is a part of her British culture. Rhianon, part Scottish, part British, was born in South Africa and immigrated to Canada at age nine.

< 237 >

Sherree Clark: I have been writing stories and poems for as long as I can remember. I have "retired" from my nine-to-five job as a therapist due to my disability and can now devote more time to my two loves, art and writing. As a writer and an artist I believe very strongly in using my words and hands to resurrect myself, women's myths and everyday events to tell present-day stories, especially where the myth may empower and lend strength to the images of disabled women. My poetry also allows me to say things I might not otherwise have the opportunity to voice, and in so doing it helps me to work out personal and public issues related to being disabled in a non-accepting and disabling society.

Lisa Comeau: I am a working-class white lesbian single mother disabled with Chronic Fatigue Syndrome and Environmental Illness. I have performed action poetry, done theatre, organized women's events, read at many poetry venues, written scripts and I am working on a poetry manuscript. There is an uncertainty and sense of groundlessness that comes with reduced choices and countless limits. When we do the best we can in sometimes stultifying conditions, a fragile sense of strength and wholeness can result. This is survival. My work explores this difficult and challenging territory.

Vicky D'Auost is still deciding what map to follow to get to the territory she is already at. Her daughter is growing into a tall and beautiful woman, and has learned from her mother to talk back, question authority and do the right thing — the thing thats right for her. As a teacher and advocate Vicky is still amazed at how much motherhood makes you teach and advocate and how hard it is to face peoples labels and judgement. She thanks LAP for being a good navigator through the rough terrain.

magie dominic is a Canadian writer and artist living in New York. She is a member of the League of Canadian Poets. Her work has been published in numerous magazines in Canada, the United States and India. She received the Langston

< 238 >

Hughes award for poetry in 1968, has had solo and group exhibits of her art in New York and Toronto and her two-part poem "alchemy," was chosen as the words for the final movement in a piece for symphony and choir, "Visions of a Wounded Earth," by Michael Horwood, world premiere April 1996 in Ontario. She has been a feminist and a peace activist for thirty years and her work frequently centres on minorities, history and the environment. Her collaborative chapbook, "belle lettres" was published by the Feminist Caucus of the League of Canadian Poets in 1995. She believes in angels.

Jane Field is a Toronto singer/songwriter and activist for both disability rights and lesbian and gay rights. She has performed at many rallies and benefits in and around Toronto. She has recently released her first recording independently, titled *The Fishing is Free*.

Ayasha Mayr Handel is a campy asthmatic femme who has had to cope with experiences of long-term illness and environmental sensitivity. She is a collector of remains and a Women's Studies student at the University of Toronto. When she is not playing house with her partner she is busy procuring irony in the rest of her queer space.

Laura Hershey is an activist, writer, poet, and lover — not necessarily in that order. In her political work and in her writing, Hershey envisions and agitates for the human rights of all people, particularly those with disabilities. As an activist with American Disabled for Attendant Programs Today (ADAPT), Hershey participates in nonviolent direct actions to protest confinement of disabled people in nursing homes; she does community organizing and media work with ADAPT. She has been published in *Ms.* magazine, *The Progressive, Sinister Wisdom, Lesbian Contradiction, Mouth, Women and Therapy*, and *Disability Rag*, among others. As owner/operator of Access*Plus* Consulting, Hershey provides training and expertise to businesses, agencies, and persons with disabilities seeking to enhance personal and political self-determination. In 1995, Hershey was awarded an Ideas

< 239 >

Grant from the World Institute on Disability, to attend the Fourth International Non-Governmental Organizations Forum on Women in Beijing, China; and to conduct research on leadership development for women with disabilities. Hershey is a member of the Nationwide Women's Program of the American Friends Service Committee. Hershey earned a Bachelor of Arts degree in History in 1983 from Colorado College, where she graduated cum laude and was named the Outstanding History Graduate.

Daphne L. Hill: "...and I will have sex again" is one of a series of writings reflecting my experience as a woman, a lesbian and person with a disability. I had a tragic hiking accident in 1986 that left me paralysed from the waist down. I am a part-time writer, full-time therapist for persons who are chemically dependent as well as disabled. I write from my experience in hopes that it will purge my grief as well as help others purge theirs. I believe that in writing about my disability I can reclaim what is mine and show others that those of us who may appear different are not. I am interested in exploring ancient myths and fables for clues about persons with disabilities in the hopes of unravelling the stigma that exists in the present.

Frances Yip Hoi is a psychiatric survivor, writer and visual artist who is just coming out about coping with illness. Under the pseudonym *Frantic*, a photo essay entitled "At the Site of Exile" was displayed at the annual show *Art of Darkness* in 1995. A mixed media installation "Har Gow Press: Recipes of Resistance" appeared in a show by artists of mixed race descent at Arts in Action Gallery as part of Asian Heritage Month also in 1995. Her writing and artwork have appeared in *Tangled Sheets: Stories of Lesbian Lust, Everywoman's Almanac, At the Crossroads Journal, Da Juice!* and *Fireweed*. Her creative impulses usually occur during episodes of insomnia, and a penchant for speed-reading assists in her studies at the University of Toronto.

< 240 >

Jade: As a Deaf Woman of Colour, Jade feels that her experience and background led her with the sensitivities necessary to capture the essence of her community's experience on film. She was born in Jamaica, West Indies in 1965 and moved with her family to Mount Vernon, New York at the age at five where she first became deaf. At Gallaudet University in Washington, DC, Jade majored in Physical Education and minored in Fine Arts. After graduating with an Associate of Arts, Jade enroled at New York University Tisch School of the Arts. In 1993, Jade became the first Deaf African American Woman to ever enrol and graduate from Tisch School of the Arts in film. After gaining valuable experience while working with Paramount Pictures, Moving Pictures Targets, Wimmins and a Mission Productions, and other production companies, Jade founded DeafVision Filmworks, Inc. She also recently founded Jade Films Inc., a New York based for-profit commercial production company, that produces original work into low-to-medium budget motion pictures and videos for distribution to theatres, network and cable television. Currently, Jade not only serves as the President of DeafVision Filmworks and Jade Films, but she is also an active Board member for two community organizations: Deaf Women United (DWU) and Black Deaf Advocates (BDA). She believes by forming partnerships with the deaf community she can better open up the opportunities for the future.

Louise Lander is a breast-cancer survivor in her late fifties who has written books, essays, and poetry, some published, some not. She does word processing part time on the evening shift to pay the rent and travels to Latin America twice a year. An essay on her cancer experience, "Coming Out As a One-Breasted Woman," appears in the anthology *Confronting Cancer, Constructing Change: New Perspectives on Women and Cancer* edited by Midge Stocker (Chicago: Third Side Press, 1993).

< 241 >

Shemaya Mountain Laurel lives in a tiny nontoxic trailer in the woods of western Massachusetts. Her disabilities include environmental illness and both mega back and wrist problems... Though politically not satisfied with the term, "homebound" best describes the most life changing aspects of those disabilities. Shemaya hangs out, writes, bird watches, and does techie stuff like figuring out nontoxic adaptive equipment. Her house is a monument to the versatility of paper clips, clothes pins, binder clips and aluminum foil. She is still working on how to translate her former radical woods dyke self into an image she can recognize in the present day mirror.

Audre Lorde (1934-1992) was the author of ten volumes of poetry and five works of prose, including *Undersong: Chosen Poems Old and New, Our Dead Behind Us*, and the autobiography *Zami*. An internationally recognized activist and artist, Lorde's honours include the Manhattan Borough President's Award for Excellence in the Arts (1988); in 1991 she was named the New York State Poet.

Margot K. Louis lives in British Columbia and teaches at the University of Victoria. She has published poems in *Fireweed, Herspectives*, and the *Hawthorne Anthology*. She has had chronic fatigue syndrome for six years.

Andrea Lowe is a writer and photographer living in Vancouver. Ten years ago at the age of 29 she received the stunning and confusing news that she had rheumatoid arthritis. Previously healthy, strong and independent, she has had to move her life and herself in many different directions to come to terms with pain, disability and uncertainty. Her belief in holistic healing is challenging but keeps her going. She's still an amazon.

Kathleen Martindale: As a native of Brooklyn, New York, Kathleen Martindale escaped to Canada during the Vietnam War. Like many New Yorkers, Kathleen was always in touch with her anger. (Just one more myth about cancer destroyed.) A tireless advocate for many causes, she lived her politics.

< 242 >

She was actively engaged with decisions about her health care and process of dying — a process which, like the rest of her life, was honourable, courageous, intensely embraced and consumed with love. Kathleen died three years and six weeks after "Lump Day." At the time of her death, she was an associate professor of English at York University. This, the original version of her cancer narrative, was previously published in "softer form" in *Fireweed: A Feminist Quarterly of Writing, Politics, Art & Culture* and *Resist: Essays Against a Homophobic Culture* (Toronto: Women's Press, 1994). Kathleen Martindale's book, *Un/Popular Culture, Lesbian Writing After the Sex Wars*, is forthcoming from SUNY Press.

Judith Moses is a 39-year-old lesbian with Charcot Marie Tooth Syndrome, a neuromuscular disorder. She has been active in the anti-violence movement since 1978 and currently works as an independent consultant with Radical Revisioning Consulting Services. She lives alone in Kingston, Ontario.

Connie Panzarino is a 48-year-old lesbian with Spinal Muscular Atrophy II. She has maintained a psychotherapy/art therapy practice for 18 years and in May 1994 published her autobiography *The Me in the Mirror* with Seal Press. She has since published two children's books for kids with spinal cord disabilities and is working on a third one for teens. She has been an activist for disability rights since she was 24. She lives in Jamaica Plain, MA, and is single and looking.

Pat Parker, Black lesbian poet, feminist medical administrator, mother of two daughters, lover of women, softball devotee and general progressive troublemaker, lived from January 20, 1944 until she died of breast cancer on June 17, 1989 at the age of 45. Her 1978 work *Movement in Black* has recently been republished by Firebrand Books.

Mary Frances Platt is a drooling, plugged-in, wheeling radical whose anti-ableist writing has been widely published in the feminist press. She participates in creating integrated access communities and crip culture at Saguaro Sisterland in Tucson Arizona and Camp Mary in New England.

< 243 >

Pauline Rankin is a Jewish lesbian feminist currently working for the DisAbled Women's Network Canada as the editor of their newsletter "Thriving." She has a long history of working in the women's and disability movements. She writes as much as she can on an many topics as she can.

Dragonsani Renteria is a multilingual Mexican/Italian-American dyke who grew up in El Paso, Texas. For many years actively involved in the Deaf gay and lesbian community, she is an activist, filmmaker, and journalist. She is the director of the Deaf Gay and Lesbian Community Centre in San Francisco, where she currently resides. She is also the publisher and editor of *Coming Together News*. Involved in a number of organizations including the Northern California Leather Association of the Deaf, she holds a BA from the University of California at Berkeley, and will soon be working toward her degree (JD) in juvenile law.

Kathleen Rockhill is on the faculty of the Ontario Institute of Studies in Education, University of Toronto. In her research and writing, she has worked to develop an integrated analysis of race, sexuality, class and ethnicity in constituting im/possibility for women. She is particularly interested in autobiography as an approach to critical inquiry, and is writing a book on the topic. Body permitting, Kathleen anticipates future research and writing on sexuality and disability.

Barbara Ruth a.k.a. Miriam Inanna Bat Dharma is yer typical anarcha-Lesbian-feminist Potowatomee-Jewish Buddhist with Sufi, Hindu and Wiccan tendencies. Oh, you know the type. She lives in California, USA, about an hour from exotic terrain.

Sherry Shute is a Toronto-based electric guitarist, who has played with everyone from Lillian Allen to David Ramsden to Robert Priest to Faith Nolan. Her lead guitar has been a driving force behind many of Toronto's truly outstanding bands over the years. She graduated from the prestigious Musicians' Institute (GIT) in Los Angeles, with honours in

< 244 >

1990. While she has suffered significant loss of ambulatory ability to Multiple Sclerosis, her guitar playing and songwriting continue to thrive. Sherry has just released the "double" (two songs on each side) *A Double Shot of Sherry* on which "Lost in the Swamp" appears. She is currently working toward recording a full-length album.

Allison Sletcher is a Celtic Lesbian woman living and creating in Toronto. She uses the medium of batik to present images of women and the medium of pen and ink to design body tattoos. Her work emphasizes emotional expression through the body. Having experienced years of illness, her art challenges myths of illness and disability by presenting positive body images. Some of the last remaining history of the red-headed Pictish People is Celtic design. The Picts lived an oral existence in Northern Britain and Scotland before Roman invasion. The history of the Pictish people is scattered amongst Scottish folklore. Known to go out into battle naked with blue designs painted on their bodies, the Picts sent the Romans running at first sight — the courage of the spirit being greater than metal, wood, stone and cloth. What remains of Pictish history besides Celtic design is stereotyped portraits created by the Romans and Saxons of a "barbarian" people.

Mickey Spencer: My poem "Caretaker Nightmares" is part of a series of the same name about caretaking from a recipient's point of view. (I know the correct term is "caregiver" but this series is about caretakers.) The series consists of nine paintings, this poem, and a short narrative. I became chronically ill over twenty years ago when I was in my early forties, and my life has become increasingly limited as my symptoms progress. For fifteen years, I co-edited *Broomstick*, an anti-agist feminist journal. We discontinued publication in December 1993. Since then, I have devoted most of my creative and political energy to painting and writing. Although I already need help with many things, and am likely to need more help as time goes on, I want to do as much as I can for myself, for as long as I am able. So these paintings

< 245 >

and writings depict some of my nightmares — visions of how things could be as I lose more of my capacities. In addition to disability and age, my political and creative activities also deal with issues around being Jewish, fat, and a lesbian. I also try not to ignore the effects of my white middle-class privileges.

Shahnaz Stri: I am a South Asian woman with a disability. I am also studying to get into medicine and Arabic at the University of Toronto (It's hell!!! No one has any sense of politics!!!) I was born in India and came to Canada in 1976. I have been writing practically all my life. I enjoy playing the occasional game of bingo and singing in the shower.

Patrizia Tavormina is a Sicilian-Canadian feminist, dyke, activist, instigator, who enjoys eating "cavatuni" and "milingiani," and plotting to overthrow oppressive establishments (in line with her ancestors).

Two Feathers is a Native activist of the Cayuga Nation, fighting all forms of injustices against all oppressed people. A short story writer and poet, she is also a member of Women's Action Against Racist Policing, the Camp SIS Collective, and the Indigenous Women's Coalition.

zana: i am 49, jewish, and disabled with arthritis, scoliosis, chronic fatigue and chemical sensitivities. i've lived on land with other lesbians for 16 years. it's not easy! having the wildness of nature in my daily life brings joy, wisdom, inspiration. a collection of my poetry and art, *herb womon*, is available for $7 (postpaid to usa and canada) from me at the HC2 box 6872-44, tucson, az 85735, usa.

< 246 >

Photo by Moe Laverty

Shelley Tremain is writing a doctoral dissertation on disablement and social justice in the Philosophy Department of York
University (Toronto, Canada). In 1993, she co-ordinated
POSTER KIDS NO MORE — a multidisciplinary programme of
visual art, readings, and music by disabled dykes — for A Space
Gallery, an artist-run centre in Toronto. A working-class, anti-
ableist activist, Shelley has produced radio programming on
disabled dykes for CKLN-FM 88.1, a politically progressive
community radio station in Toronto, and was integral to the
development of an anti-ableist publishing policy at Women's
Press (Toronto). She is the editor of *Bodies of Knowledge:
Critical Perspectives on Disablement and Disabled Women*, a
collection of essays by disabled feminist activists, community
workers and academics (Toronto: Women's Press, forthcoming).